Scituate
and the
Civil War

By Lynn K. Sheridan
With Elizabeth M. Foster
and Florence Mehegan Ely

The information provided within this book is for general informational purposes only. While we try to keep the information up-to-date and correct, there are no representations or warranties, express or implied, about the completeness, accuracy, reliability, suitability or availability with respect to the information, products, services, or related graphics contained in this book for any purpose.

Reproduction of this book in any form is strictly prohibited without the written consent of the publisher.

ISBN: 978-0-9910923-4-5
Copyright © The Scituate Town Archives

Published in 2018 by:
Converpage
23 Acorn Street
Scituate, MA 02066

Dedication

For George Bailey, who survived the war, Andersonville prison, and the Florence Stockade and for my father and grandfather, who were dedicated to researching and preserving the family Civil War history. L.K.S.

To Walter Foster 2nd and his son Charles A. Foster. Both were born in Scituate and enlisted from South Scituate. Only one, unfortunately, survived. E.M.F.

For the courageous and determined women on the Civil War home front, who, over 150 years later, continue to inspire us to "do small things with great love." *Mother Teresa* F.M.E.

Acknowledgements

An undertaking such as this one depends upon the efforts of many people. The authors wish to thank the volunteers at the Scituate Town Archives, especially Pat Jones, who with much humor and patience helped to transcribe the fading words of historical documents, and Maureen Alcott, who searched through an immense amount of material looking for any bit of information from the Civil War for this project. Special thanks goes to Beryl Denker and Susan Kasper for sharing artifacts, letters, and photographs. The assistance and guidance of Carol Miles and Mary Porter at The Scituate Historical Society were extremely helpful in locating photographs and letters. We are grateful for the copy-editing skills of Ed Leary and his encouragement of this endeavor. We would like to also thank Pam McCallum, who is not only our publisher, but also a dedicated researcher and friend that helped to keep this project moving forward. Special thanks to the Scituate Community Preservation Committee who generously supplied the funds for this publication. We are indebted to the men and women of Scituate who recorded and preserved the town documents for future generations. Finally, we want to express gratitude to those that served in the Civil War and to the people of Scituate who supported them.

Scituate and the Civil War
Contents

Acknowledgements	1
Preface	5
Part I: Scituate and the Civil War by Lynn K. Sheridan	
1. Call to Arms	9
2. The Town of Scituate	13
3. The Years Leading to the Civil War	19
4. 1861: The Civil War Begins	29
5. 1862: Ladies Assoc. and Letters Home	33
6. 1863: Calls for Soldiers and the Draft	51
7. 1864: Scituate Sailors and Filling Quota	59
8. 1865: The Civil War Ends	73
9. Notes	79
Part II: The Grand Army of the Republic Post No. 31 by Florence Mehegan Ely	83
Part III: The Monument to the Soldiers and Sailors by Elizabeth M. Foster	89
Part IV: Waldo Turner Letters	97
Part V: List of Scituate Soldier and Sailors	105
Selected Bibliography	157

COMPLETE

RECORD OF THE NAMES

OF ALL THE

SOLDIERS AND OFFICERS

IN THE MILITARY SERVICE,

AND OF ALL THE

SEAMEN AND OFFICERS

IN THE NAVAL SERVICE

OF THE UNITED STATES,

FROM

The Town of Scituate, in Plymouth County, Massachusetts

DURING THE REBELLION BEGUN IN 1861:

TOGETHER WITH

AUTHENTIC FACTS RELATING TO THE MILITARY OR NAVAL CAREER OF EACH SOLDIER, SEAMAN, AND OFFICER.

MADE OUT, WITH ADDITIONS FROM TIME TO TIME, IN CONFORMITY WITH THE STATUTES OF THE COMMONWEALTH, APPROVED MARCH 7, 1864, AND APRIL 29, 1865.

Volume 1.

RECORD BOOK SUPPLIED BY GEORGE COOLIDGE, 3 MILK STREET, BOSTON.

Entered, according to Act of Congress, in the year 1865, by George Coolidge, in the Clerk's Office of the District Court of the District of Massachusetts.

Scituate and the Civil War

PREFACE

Every good project begins with a question. This project started when a leather bound book that had been patiently waiting on the shelf of the town's archives was opened: *The Complete Record of the Names of all the Soldiers and Officers in the Military Service and of all the Seamen and Officers in the Naval Service of the United States from the Town of Scituate in Plymouth County, Massachusetts During the Rebellion Begun in 1861* (henceforth referred to as *Scituate's Record of Names*). The book holds pages and pages of names that were carefully written down over 150 years ago. There were over two hundred and forty names in the book. Who were these men that served in the Civil War? The majority of the men were born and resided in Scituate; some men lived and worked here for only a short time, while others living in nearby towns helped to fill Scituate's quota for soldiers. A few men on the list never set foot in Scituate. In most cases, next to each name is listed their birth date, occupation, if they were married or single and sometimes even the name of their parents. The next question arose naturally: Did they survive the bloody battles that tore the nation apart?

The Civil War is an immense and complicated part of American history; there are hundreds of books documenting and analyzing the war and its battles. This book does not attempt to be an expert on the Civil War, but rather it looks at the years leading up to and during the Civil War through the lens of the small seaside town of Scituate, Massachusetts. How did the townspeople respond to the national turmoil over slavery? How did the inhabitants of Scituate cope with the continuous calls from President Lincoln and Congress for more soldiers? In what ways did the people of Scituate honor those that served?

One question led to another, and the real work began, trying to find the voices from long ago through words written in primary sources. At first there was a fleeting thought that one box existed, containing all the information, but the reality is that there are bits and pieces scattered throughout basements, backrooms, personal collections, public records, and filing cabinets. One hundred and fifty years was a very long time ago, and any information discovered is truly a gift.

One path of investigation led to the newspapers of the time. For example, *The Scituate Herald* newspaper was first published in 1859, and there were hopes that this would be an abundant source of information; unfortunately, it was a challenge to locate any surviving issues of the paper. In fact, only one edition was found: Volume 1, No. 47, dated January 19, 1860 at the American Antiquarian Society in Worcester Massachusetts. As disappointing as this may have seemed at the time, it led to the discovery that a Scituate resident had written a powerful letter to William Lloyd Garrison, the editor of the abolitionist newspaper, *The Liberator* (January 4, 1861 edition). The search extended to neighboring towns, looking for any newspaper articles about Scituate during these tumultuous times. Fortunately, the Hingham Library has *The Hingham Journal and South Shore Advertiser* for the years 1861 through 1865 on microfiche. Usually on page two of every Friday's edition included a section called "Town and Vicinity," in which news from a correspondent in Scituate occasionally appeared.

Other primary sources included the aforementioned *Scituate Record of Names*, eight volumes of *The Massachusetts Soldiers, Sailors, and Marines in the Civil War* (compiled and published in 1930's by the Adjutant General), town meetings, the Selectmen records, the annual town reports, the School Committee reports, General Orders from the Commonwealth of Massachusetts, correspondence with records of the Grand Army of the Republic Post No. 31, the local Provost Marshall's office, actual soldiers' letters home, and the minutes of the Ladies Sanitary Association. All give us a glimpse back in time. The best effort was made to have an accurate list of the soldiers and sailors who served for the town and to gather some information for each of them; however, even when using all these primary and secondary sources, there were times when data were incomplete, or non-existent due to the difficult nature of acquiring accurate documentation from that period.

We are indebted to the many volunteers in both the Scituate Town Archives and Scituate Historical Society who have been committed to the preservation and protection of historical documents and historical sites of this town. It is our hope that this book will provide a starting point for further research on the men who served in the Civil War and the townspeople who supported them.

Lynn K. Sheridan
Scituate, Massachusetts
2018

Part I
Scituate and the Civil War
By Lynn K. Sheridan

CHAPTER 1

CALL TO ARMS

For months in 1861, Confederate militiamen had surrounded Fort Sumter, a Federal fort in South Carolina's Charleston Harbor, in order to deny both provisions and reinforcements to the soldiers within its stone walls. In the early morning of April 12, 1861, Confederate gunners fired upon the fort, signaling the beginning of the bloody conflict that would tear this country apart. The news of the assault soon flooded into every town and city in the country. On April 15, 1861, President Abraham Lincoln responded by issuing a proclamation calling for a militia of 75,000 men to serve ninety days, "appeal(ing) to all loyal citizens to favor, facilitate, and aid this effort to maintain the honor, the integrity, and the existence of our National Union and the perpetuity of popular government and to redress wrongs already long enough endured."[1]
As was the case throughout the country, the men in the small

seaside town of Scituate, Massachusetts twenty-five miles south of Boston immediately lined up and volunteered to serve. John Peak Cushing was the first to enlist in Scituate, mustering into Company A of the 8th Regiment Massachusetts Volunteer Infantry. His name appeared in many other local documents during the Civil War period, and John Peak Cushing was the last soldier mentioned in the minutes of the Scituate Ladies Sanitary Association on September 26, 1865. He was born in Scituate on March 19, 1836, to parents Nathaniel and Olive (Wade) and like his father, worked as a blacksmith. His became the very first of the more than 240 names entered in the aforementioned *Scituate's Record of Names,* a total that is truly amazing, given the fact that the 1860 militia list notes that there were only 300 men between the ages of eighteen and forty-five years living in Scituate at the time. The townspeople's overwhelming support of the war effort was captured in the "Town and Vicinity" section of a neighboring town's newspaper, *The Hingham Journal and South Shore Advertiser,* on Friday April 26, 1861, (Vol. 12 No. 17).

> Our Scituate correspondent writes that a large and spirited meeting was held at the Town Hall in that town on Monday evening last to take measures to raise a Volunteer Company for immediate service. Seth Webb Jr., Esq., headed the enlistment and during the evening twenty young men volunteered. G. M. Allen and S. Webb Esqs., gave $1000 each for the support and equipment of the soldiers and their families. The meeting also voted to call a Town Meeting to raise money for the same purpose. Also that another Company be raised for home service and drill. Several patriotic songs were sung, and the meeting adjourned to Thursday evening. We have heard from the Herald that Hon. C. W. Prouty, the well known and popular County Commissioner of this section of the County, is organizing a Coast Guard.

Every time that the President and Congress issued a call for volunteers, each state would be assigned a quota, a specific number of men that must be raised for military service; by order of Governor John A. Andrews and Adjutant General Wm. Schouler, each city or town in Massachusetts was assigned their portion of the quota. Whenever a new order arrived at Town Hall, the men of Scituate were ready to serve. The volunteers, who knew the thunderous sound of waves crashing against the rocky shore and the calls of seagulls, would soon know the rumble of battle and the cries of the injured and dying on the battlefield. Some would never return to their town by the sea, buried instead in graves far from home.

CHAPTER 2

THE TOWN OF SCITUATE

The town of Scituate was founded in 1636, long before there was a United States of America. In his *History of Scituate, Massachusetts, From its Settlement to 1831,* Samuel Deane noted that:

> The Pilgrims of Plymouth explored the shores very early after their landing, and took notice of the eligible places for settlement. It is certain that William Gillson, Anthony Annable, Thomas Bird, Nathaniel Tilden, Edward Foster, Henry Rowley, and some others were here before 1628. The above named gentlemen and others, were called 'men of Kent' having come from that County in England.[2]

Over 200 years later, in 1860 there were 2,227 residents. The light of the Scituate Lighthouse in the harbor had been extinguished in September of that year because the newly-restored Minot's Lighthouse once again stood among the off-shore ledges to the north. The

Courtesy of The Scituate Historical Society.

tides rose and fell along the town's twelve miles of rocky and sandy shoreline. The four cliffs south of town were still connected, and the mouth of the North River opened three miles south of its current location; it would be years before the storm of 1898 washed away the barrier beach between Third and Fourth Cliff, creating a new mouth for the river.

The white oak and white pine that had once thickly grown nearly to the coastline had long been cleared and used for local shipbuilding. In fact, shipyards on the North River and Scituate Harbor had built over a thousand ships: merchantmen, whalers and coasters.[3] By 1860, however, the wooden shipbuilding industry had nearly ended, as the wood supply diminished and the construction of steam powered vessels increased.

The industrial statistics of May 1, 1865, were included in the *Report of the Selectmen on the Financial Affairs of the Town of Scituate for the Year Ending March 4, 1866* give some insight into the economic activities of the time. For example, the "Products of the Sea" section documented that 3,153 bbls. (barrels) of herring, 123,000 lobsters, 441 quintals of codfish, and 40 bbls. (barrels) of mackerel were sold. Mechanical products made in Scituate included needlework, stove polish, ironwork, boats, tin ware and stoves.

New industries also provided employment for the area. The report reveals that shoe manufacturing was expanding with factories not only in nearby towns but also in Scituate, with 66,745 pairs of boots and shoes produced at a value of $142,811. Furthermore Scituate's waters proved to be a successful location for the Irish Mossing Industry, which started in the 1850's by Irish immigrants. A line item in "Products of the Sea" stated that 465,980 lbs. of moss had been harvested, with a value of $22,558. Mossers would set off in dories as the waters neared low tide of Scituate Harbor, Sand Hills and Peggotty Beach. Using long rakes, the mossers pulled the seaweed from rocks into the boats.

The heavy sea moss would then be spread out on the smoothed beach above the high tide line to dry, rinsed with salt water and dried again until fully bleached. The cured moss, carrageenan, was sold to be used in medicines, toothpaste, foods, and soaps.[4]

Farming was a staple in Scituate. The "products of 408 gardens" had a value of $8,471. There were also larger farms growing fields of potatoes, onions, turnips, barley, rye, English hay, and fresh meadow hay. Salt meadow hay was harvested from the marshes. Animal products included eggs, butter, wool, and milk, as well as beef, pork, poultry, mutton, and veal.

The 1865 statistics also recorded the number of livestock as 255 horses, 138 oxen over four years old, 80 steers under four years old, 360 milking cows, 56 heifers, and 658 sheep. The Pound Keeper and three Fence Viewers ensured that stray animals were penned and that fences were kept in good order. There were seventeen Surveyors of Highway in charge of building new roads and maintaining roads worn by horses and other animals, wagon wheels, weather, and the inevitable high tides. Local businesses, merchants, churches, schoolhouses, a town hall and 496 houses filled in the landscape of the town.

The *Report of The School Committee for the Year Ending March 1, 1861*, counted 453 children between the ages of five and fifteen living in Scituate. An outbreak of measles swept through the town in the

Courtesy of The Scituate Historical Society.

During the Civil War years, classes were held for older students at Town Hall (at right above).

spring of 1860, causing attendance at the schools to be lower than usual. A Central Grammar School had recently opened at Town Hall, for the older and more advanced pupils, and there were ten Primary Schools Houses throughout the town: Harbor School, Common Street School, Willow Street School, Egypt School, Neck School, North Main Street School, Greenbush School, Centre School, Grove Street School, and West School. In the school report that year, Mrs. Mary L. G. Beale, a teacher at the Harbor School, received praise for:

> The progress of some of the scholars from the Cliffs was noteworthy. In other branches the classes were made to understand their lessons, the teacher not being satisfied with a simple memorizing. The classes in Arithmetic need, perhaps, a little more thorough drilling. The order was usually good, and the School as quiet as we could expect for so large a Primary School.

Mr. Henry S. Bates taught at the newly-formed Central Grammar School. The School Committee felt that he was "particular adapted to the work of teaching [but] the School in the Summer was composed of scholars from all parts of the Town, unaccustomed to attending School together; and, consequent upon this new arrangement, there were many habits to be broken, and new habits to form." The Primary school teachers were paid $16 or $18 a month. George C. Lee, Esq., taught the winter session at North Main Street School and was paid $25 each month, and the teacher of the Central Grammar School was paid $48 a month. School Committee members Thomas T. Bailey, George M. Allen, and Thomas Clapp recommended that the town reduce the number of Primary School Houses and have a few schools comprising both Primary and Grammar "with the ultimate view of a High School." The Committee noted, "this may be considered by some impracticable in some of our sparsely populated Districts; but in our opinion, children can go much farther to school than is generally supposed." In the Central School many of the students that attended regularly "lived at the distance of two miles or upward from the Hall."

During this time the Selectmen Records included correspondence with the selectmen of neighboring towns, setting a time and date for perambulating the town lines. They would walk the town lines and confirm that the stone monuments erected to mark the lines were still standing and in the correct position. It was noted that the Scituate and Cohasset Selectmen had plans to meet at Waterman Bailey's store in Cohasset before beginning their task.

The town of South Scituate, which had originally been part of Scituate, split to become its own town in 1849 and was later renamed Norwell after a prominent local merchant. The South Shore Railroad ran from the Cohasset and Hingham train stations into Boston twice a day. An advertisement in *The Hingham Journal and South Shore Advertiser* announced that for twenty-five cents the steamer Nantasket carried passengers from Hingham to Liverpool Wharf in Boston. Local horse-drawn stagecoaches drove Scituate residents to the train and steamboat. The "Post Roads and Tavern" chapter of the book, *Old Scituate*, stated, "during the days of the Civil War the traffic was very heavy, and two coaches were needed each day."[5]

CHAPTER 3

THE YEARS LEADING TO THE CIVIL WAR

In the decades prior to the Civil War, the unity of the United States of America was tested, as tension between the Northern and Southern states over the issue of slavery grew sharper. In 1820 the Missouri Compromise ruled that of the new land acquired by the Louisiana Purchase, only Missouri would be admitted as a slave state, and no new slave states would be permitted north of the parallel that marked Missouri's southern border. Thirty years later, the Compromise of 1850 tried to smooth the waves of conflict that surfaced over the controversy of slavery spreading into the new territories acquired after the Mexican-American War. Anti-slavery advocates expected the new territories to prohibit slavery, while pro-slavery groups demanded that slave owners had the right to bring all of their possessions, including slaves, into the territories. In the end, California was admitted as a free state; the territories of New Mexico and Utah would determine their status by popular sovereignty, and the slave trade ended in the District of Columbia. The Compromise of 1850 also included a revised Fugitive Slave Act, which denied anyone accused of being a runaway slave the right to a hearing, and in fact required law enforcement to return runaway slaves to slave owners.

Massachusetts took steps toward banning slavery many years earlier due in large part to the ruling in 1783 of the Commonwealth vs. Jennison. In his instructions to the jury Scituate native, William Cushing, Chief Justice of the Massachusetts Supreme Judicial Court argued that:

> Our Constitution of Government, by which the people of the Commonwealth have solemnly bound themselves, sets out with declaring that all men are born free and equal, and that every subject is entitled to liberty and to have it guarded by the laws, as well as life and property; and, in short, is totally repugnant to the idea of being born slaves...the idea of slavery is inconsistent with our own conduct and Constitution.[6]

George Washington later nominated William Cushing to be a Justice of the United States Supreme Court, where he served over twenty years. He was offered the position of Chief Justice, which he declined due to poor health.

The inhabitants of Scituate continued to vote against slavery. In the pages of the *Town of Scituate's Book of Records of Town Meetings* dated Monday April 7, 1851, the following resolutions were recorded:

> Voted – To accept as the sense of this meeting by a vote of 90 to 34 the following Resolutions
>
> Whereas, there are thousands of the citizens of Massachusetts, liable at any moment to be kidnapped into Slavery, an institution the infamy of which is so broad, that human thought in vain attempts its span: so deep, that no fathom line has ever sounded its hideous abyss: so high, that even Heaven shudders at its proximity:—
>
> And whereas, the Law, aiding in kidnapping in the eyes of all eminent lawyers, providing that eminence is based in integrity and humanity (by refusing the trial by jury in the State where the seizure takes place, and in annulling the right to the writ of "Habeus Corpus") is clearly and undeniably unconstitutional:—
>
> And Whereas, the Massachusetts Bill of Rights, in declaring that all men are created free and equal, and endowed by their Creator with an inalienable right to liberty, strikes the fetters from off every person within the limits of the State guilty of no crime:—
>
> Therefore, Resolved 1st. that poverty has no crust however mouldy, nor the dungeon any cell however gloomy that the citizens of Scituate shall refuse to eat the one, or enter the other before they will assist the Slavehunter in sending his prey to that "prison house of horrors," the plantation of the Slave States.
>
> Resolved 2nd. That as kidnapping in Massachusetts is as criminal as it is in Congo, it should be made commensurately penal.
>
> Resolved 3rd. That the Bill recently introduced into the Senate by the Hon. Mr. Buckingham, securing to all the citizens of Massachusetts the right of trial by jury, and rendering effective the right to the writ of "Habeus Corpus," should, as it doubtless will receive the support of every Legislator in General Court assembled, who endeavours to incorporate the precepts of Christianity into the Statute Book.
>
> A True Copy Attest
> Edward James, Town Clerk

Courtesy of The Scituate Town Archives.

Voted - To accept as the sense of this meeting by a vote of 90 to 34 the following Resolutions

Whereas, there are thousands of citizens of Massachusetts liable at any moment to be kidnapped into Slavery, an institution the infamy of which is so broad, that human thought in vain attempts its span; so deep, that no fathom line has ever sounded its hideous abyss; so high, that even Heaven shudders at its proximity

And whereas, the <u>Law</u>, aiding in kidnapping in the eyes of all eminent lawyers, providing that eminence is based in integrity and humanity (by refusing the trial by jury in the State where the seizure takes place and in annulling the right to the writ of "Habeas Corpus") is clearly and undeniably unconstitutional!-

And whereas, the Massachusetts Bill of Rights, in declaring that all men are created free and equal, and endowed by this Creator with an inalienable right to liberty, strike the fetters from off every person within the limits of the state guilty of no crime;-

Therefore, Resolved 1st that poverty has no crust however mouldy [sic], nor the dungeon any cell however gloomy that the citizens of Scituate shall refuse to eat the one, or enter the other before they will assist the Slave hunters in sending his prey to that "prison house of horrors," the plantation of the Southern States.

Resolved 2d, That a kidnapping in Massachusetts is as criminal as it is in Congo, it should be made commensurately penal,

Resolved 3d, That the Bill recently introduced into the Senate by the Hon. Mr. Buckingham, securing to all the citizens of Massachusetts the right of trial by jury, and rendering effective the right to the writ of "Habeas Corpus," should as it doubtless will receive the support of every Legislator in the General Court assembled, who endeavors to incorporate the precept of Christianity into the Statute Book.
    A True Copy Attest
     Edward James} Town Clerk

Courtesy of The Scituate Historical Society.

As Congress debated the Kansas-Nebraska Act in the spring of 1854, the citizens of Scituate made their views on the subject abundantly clear at the town meetings from March 6, 1854, to April 3, 1854. Town Clerk J. O. Cole recorded the meetings.

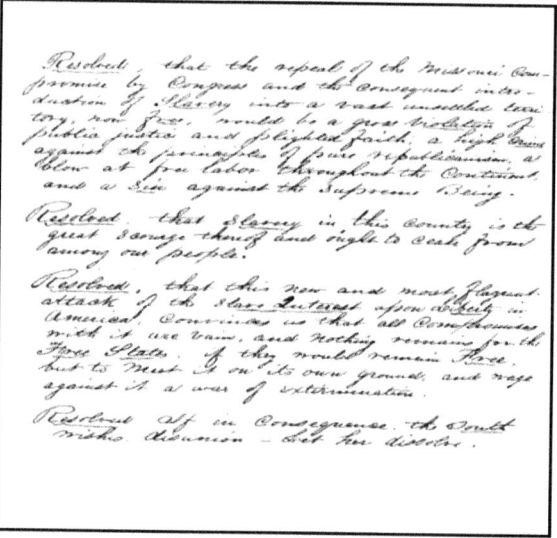

Courtesy of The Scituate Town Archives.

Resolved, that the repeal of the Missouri Compromise by Congress and the consequent introduction of Slavery into a vast unsettled territory, now free, would be a gross violation of public justice and plighted faith, a high crime against the principles of pure republicanism, a blow at free labor throughout the continent, and a sin against the Supreme Being.

Resolved, that slavery in this country is the great scourge thereof and ought to cease from among our people.

Resolved, that this new and most flagrant attack of the Slave Interest upon Liberty in America, convinces us that all Compromises with it are vain and nothing remains for the <u>Free States</u>, if they

would remain <u>Free</u>, but to meet it on its own grounds, and wage against it a war of extermination.

<u>Resolved</u>, If in consequence the south wishes disunion – Let her dissolve.

The voting members of the town of Scituate voted to accept the resolutions and to send a copy of the resolutions to their representatives in Congress. However, on May 30, 1854, Congress passed the Kansas-Nebraska Act, which repealed the Missouri Compromise and gave newly formed states and territories the right to choose to permit or exclude slavery. In 1857, the Supreme Court delivered another blow to the anti-slavery movement when it ruled in Scott vs. Sanford that slaves were not citizens but property and therefore had no rights.

On Tuesday, November 6, 1860, citizens who were qualified to vote in elections met at Scituate Town Hall for the purpose of voting for the President and Vice President of the United States, Governor, and other state positions.

The following votes were recorded in the *Book of Records of Town Meetings* by the Town Clerk: Lincoln and Hamlin of the Republican Party received 269 votes, Bell and Everett from the Constitutional Union Party had 82 votes, Douglas and Johnson of the Democratic Party received 52 votes, and Breckenridge and Lane representing the Southern Democratic Party had 3 votes. For the Governor of Massachusetts, John A. Andrew of Boston received 270 votes. The national election resulted in the election of Abraham Lincoln as President and Hannibal Hamlin as Vice President. John A. Andrew was elected Governor of the Commonwealth of Massachusetts.

The election of the Republican candidate, Abraham Lincoln, gave new hope to the anti-slavery movement. However, the southern states began to follow through on their threats of secession. On December 20, 1860, South Carolina seceded. The people of Scituate, as well as the citizens of the rest of the country, did not fully understand the fragile nature of the words, "The United States of America". As fall turned into winter, the nation was literally pulling apart, and the Civil War was waiting around the corner.

In the January 4, 1861, edition of *The Liberator,* an abolitionist newspaper published in Boston by William Lloyd Garrison, appeared a letter from William G. Babcock, who served as Minister of the Unitarian First Parish of Scituate from 1860 to 1865. The letter begins with salutation, "Dear Friend Garrison" and continues on to denounce the slavery:

> *Our fathers, in framing the Constitution, swerved from the right, when they demanded the free States to take part in enslaving our fellow-creatures, by delivering the fleeing bondman to his pursuer; and no permanent peace nor prosperity can bless our native land till she changes her contract on the subject Better, far better, that the North and South should be separate confederacies than we continue to perpetuate this wrong; and best of all, that the States be preserved in Union by a National Convention to amend the Constitution, by striking out the unrighteous provision to deliver up the fleeing slave. We are in favor of the Union, not only of our States, but all the nations of the world; but not of a contract to perpetuate the horrid sin of slavery; and God will see to it that, sooner or later, a Personal Liberty Bill shall be enacted and observed in every State of the Union. Massachusetts may or may not stand in the coming and the future conflicts between freedom and slavery,*

righteousness and unrighteousness; but there are individuals who will remain steadfast, till what our Governor says of the State shall hold good and true for the whole country. W.G.B.[7]

By the winter of 1861 the country had divided. Seven states had seceded, and Jefferson Davis had been inaugurated as President of the Confederacy. On March 4, 1861, President Abraham Lincoln's Inaugural Address spoke to all the people of the divided country:

> In your hands, my dissatisfied fellow countrymen, and not in mine, is the momentous issue of civil war. The government will not assail you. You can have no conflict without being yourselves the aggressors. You have no oath registered in Heaven to destroy the Government, while I shall have the most solemn one to "preserve, protect, and defend" it. I am loath to close. We are not enemies, but friends. We must not be enemies. Though passion may have strained, it must not break our bonds of affection. The mystic chords of memory, stretching from every battle-field, and patriot grave to every living heart and hearthstone, all over this broad land, will yet swell the chorus of the Union, when again touched, as surely they will be, by the better angels of our nature.[8]

CHAPTER 4

1861: THE CIVIL WAR BEGINS

In the spring of 1861 no one knew what lay ahead. The Union and Confederate leaders both thought they would quickly succeed. Unfortunately, that was far from true, for America's Civil War had begun. The people of the broken country would be pulled into the depths of turbulent times, where they would stay longer than anyone could have ever imagined. The war lasted four years with devastating consequences. In the Union army, there were 110,100 soldiers killed in battle, 224,580 soldiers that died from diseases, 30,218 soldiers that died as prisoners of war and 275,174 that were wounded in action. In the Confederate army, 94,000 soldiers were killed in battle, 164,000 soldiers died from diseases, 25,976 died as prisoners of war and over 194,026 were wounded in action.[9]

During the months before the Civil War the town meetings of Scituate were primarily focused on issues related to supporting the town's poor, schools, roads, and bridges. At the annual town meeting on March 4, 1861, the new town officers were voted into office. Edward James, Esq., was Moderator of the meeting. James

L. Merritt was chosen as Town Clerk, and three men were elected to serve as the Selectmen of Scituate: George M. Allen, Hubbard Litchfield, and George E. Cole. On this day the following positions were also filled: seventeen Surveyors of Highway, nine Field Drivers, three Fence Viewers, two Fire Wardens, a Pound Keeper, four Surveyors of Lumber and five Constables: Henry Brown, George W. Merritt, Joseph O. Cole, Enoch Gardner, and Edward James.

One of the Constables' responsibilities, in addition to maintaining law and order, was to officially notify the citizens of the town of all public meetings. For every town meeting the Selectmen wrote an official notice, called a Warrant, that stated the day, time and place of the upcoming town meeting and a list of articles that would be presented. The Constables were instructed to post a copy of the notice in all public houses seven days prior to the meeting.

On April 26, 1861, the Selectmen sent a letter to the Constables in regards to the town meeting planned for May 4, 1861. However, before the town meeting could take place, on May 3, 1861, President Lincoln called for 42,034 more volunteers, to serve three years in the infantry and cavalry, and 18,000 to serve in the United States Navy in Proclamation 83.[10] The quota for Massachusetts was six infantry regiments.[11] As a result, twenty-six men from Scituate enlisted and were mustered in June 15, 1861, into the 7th Regiment, Company K or F. Each regiment had about 1,000 men divided up in ten companies. Each company had a captain, one 1st lieutenant, one 2nd lieutenant, one 1st sergeant, three sergeants, eight corporals, two musicians, one wagoner and eighty-two privates.[12]

The town meeting did take place at Town Hall that Saturday, May 4th 1861. Town Clerk James L. Merritt recorded the meeting. It was "Voted-To pay to each volunteer soldier raised in this town, and being an inhabitant therein, and mustered into the service of the United States for the defence of the Government the following sums viz. to each soldier (except Commissioned officers and 1st and 2nd Sergeant) having a family fifteen dollars pr month in addition to the sum allowed by the United States per month and during such service and to each soldier not having a family the sum of ten dollars pr month for like service." That day, meeting members voted to give soldiers of the town up to ten dollars for a uniform and "$1.00 per day for each and every day he is drilled under proper authority" and to raise $300 for the organization of a military company in this town. The voting members of the town of Scituate voted "that the Selectmen be instructed to purchase a suitable Flag for the town and cause the same to be hoisted on the Town Hall."

Scituate held out hope that the country would soon be reunited, as celebrations for the Fourth of July were planned. *The Hingham Journal and South Shore Advertiser* June 28, 1861, Vol. 12 No. 26 noted the following items:

> Fourth of July. There is a celebration of the coming Fourth by the Band of Hope of Scituate together with all the children in town.... Scituate Volunteers. Some twenty-three of our young men belong to Capt. Harlow's Company, S. Abington, and are now at Camp Old Colony. Several of them are in town on a short furlough.

Also included in the paper that day was a story about John Peak Cushing's father and their family business, "Fire. The blacksmith shop of Mr. Nathaniel Cushing of N. Scituate accidently took fire, on Thursday the 20th inst., and was entirely consumed. Insured for $160."

John Peak Cushing was mustered out of service on August 1, 1861, in Boston, thereby fulfilling his ninety-day enlistment. In *The Hingham Journal and South Shore Advertiser* Vol. 12 No. 32 on August 9, 1861, a letter from Scituate described the celebration upon his return:

North Scituate, Aug 7th, 1861

Messrs. Editors:- Our generally quiet neighborhood was thrown into a high state of excitement on Monday night, by the "roll of the stirring drum," which called us not to arms but to our feet, when reaching headquarters we found the citizens formed under the membership of Joseph Gannet, Esq., and marching by the music of Maj. Couillard's drum corps, proceeded to the residence of private John Cushing, Co. A of the "gallant Eighth," where hearty cheers were given with a will, speeches delivered, and the "Glory Halle Hallelujah" was sung with good effort by Alfred Wood, after which the vast crowd dispersed, well satisfied with the reception given to one of the first Scituate boys that left their homes to fight for liberty and the Union.

On August 21, 1861, the records show that that John Peak Cushing re-enlisted in one of the new regiments, the 19th Regiment Massachusetts Volunteer Infantry, for three years. On August 24, 1861, he was promoted to corporal in Company H of this Regiment.

CHAPTER 5

1862: LADIES ASSOCIATION AND LETTERS HOME

As the war moved swiftly from weeks into months with no sign of ending, the women of Scituate formed a Ladies Sanitary Association as part of the U.S. Sanitary Commission. In the Civil War files of the Town Archives dated October 1, 1861, a letter from the U. S. Sanitary Commission described the urgent need of their work.

> Countrywomen: You are called upon to help take care of our sick and wounded soldiers and sailors. It is true that government undertakes their care, but all experience in every other country as well as our own, shows that government alone cannot completely provide for the humane treatment of those for whom the duty of providing, as well as possible, is acknowledged. Even at this period of the war, and with a much smaller portion of sick and wounded than is expected, there is much suffering, and dear lives are daily lost because the

government cannot put the right thing in the right place at the right time. No other government has ever provided as well for its soldiers so soon after the breaking out of a war of this magnitude, and yet it remains true that there is much suffering and that death unnecessarily occurs from the imperfectness of the government arrangements...a large portion of gifts of the people to the army hitherto have been wasted, or worse than wasted, because directed without knowledge or discrimination. It is only through the Commission that such gifts can reach the army with a reasonable assurance that they will be received where they will do the most good and the least harm...suggested that societies be at once formed in every neighborhood where they are not already established...that contribution boxes be placed in post offices, newspaper offices, railroad and telegraph offices, public houses, steamboats and in ferry boats, and in all other suitable places, labeled "For Our Sick and Wounded."[13]

There was a list of articles most wanted: blankets, quilts, knit woolen socks, woolen or canton flannel bed gowns, wrappers, undershirts and drawers, small hair and feather pillows for wounded limbs. It was requested that each box include a list of contents and that the freight should be paid in advance and sent to one of the six addresses listed.

The minutes of the Scituate Ladies Sanitary Association recorded that a meeting was held at Town Hall on August 5, 1862, to reorganize and choose new officers: Mrs. H. D. Allen as President, Mrs. C. Bates, Miss T. Cottle, and Mrs. W. G. Babcock as Vice Presidents, and Mrs. L. Tilden as Secretary and Treasurer. The town was divided into three divisions: Mrs. A. Curtis was in charge of the North part of town, Miss T. Cottle the Harbor, and Mrs. C. Bates (Clara Turner Bates) the West part of town.

It was "voted that all persons be invited to join this Society, by paying three cents for ladies and over three for Gentlemen" and that the officers would be a "Committee to confer with the U.S. Sanitary Commission at Boston." The Ladies Sanitary Association purchased six pounds of yarn and one piece of cotton and planned to meet every Tuesday from one o'clock to five o'clock.

Mrs. C. Bates of the West district reported on September 2, 1862, that there were fifty-three members present at the work meeting. They made four pair of drawers, thirty towels, thirty handkerchiefs, and five rolls of bandages. The Harbor district had seventy members present on September 9, 1862, and made nineteen pairs of drawers, towels, and lint.

Courtesy of the Scituate Town Archives.

On September 16, 1862, a general meeting of the Ladies Sanitary Association occurred at Town Hall, recorded by the Secretary L. Tilden.

"At a General meeting Ladies Sanitary Association Mrs. H. D. Allen, in the chair. Treasurer made her report viz cash on hand $22.72.

The president read the following communication from the U.S. Sanitary Commission acknowledging the reception of two Barrels of pickles and also a keg, also a valuable box of hospital supplies and a package containing 34 Bandages 2 Boxes Lint
Voted to tax ourselves one cent per week
Making towels, hdks and Bandages.
Number present 68.
L. Tilden Sect."

The book, *Old Scituate,* published in 1921, included information about Miss Patience Tilden, "a famous knitter, made with her own hands many pairs of woolen stockings for the soldiers. She was a great admirer of President Lincoln, and for him she knit a particularly fine pair of white woolen socks as a gift, and she had the rare pleasure of a personal acknowledgement from him."[14]

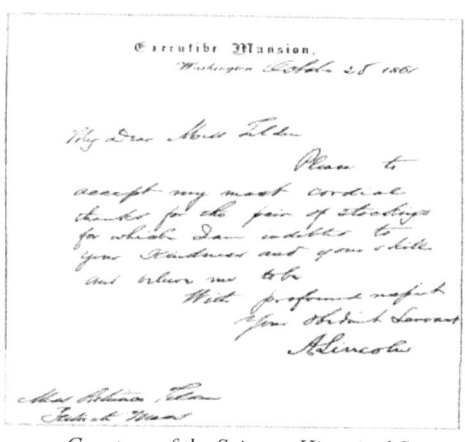

Courtesy of the Scituate Historical Society.

Calls for More Soldiers in 1862

In July 1862 an Executive Order from President Lincoln called for 300,000 men to serve in the infantry for three years.[15] Massachusetts was given a quota of 15,000 men.[16] The Town Meeting on July 21, 1862, recorded in the *Book of Records of Town Meetings*:

> Hon. C.W. Prouty offered the following Resolutions which were accepted and adopted by the town unanimously. Resolved that this town pay a bounty for $100 each in addition to the Government advance to those men who enlist in the volunteer force to furnish the quota of Scituate under the recent call of the Governor and that sum of $100 be paid to such volunteer when he shall have been mustered into the service of the United States by a proper officer. Resolved that the sum of $3000 be raised and appropriated for the above purpose and that the Treasurer be authorized to borrow the amount as needed.

As the fighting continued, it became clear that the war took much of the Selectmen's time and attention. There was also a vote at this meeting to "indefinitely postpone all other articles in the warrant relating to roads."

While the town struggled with the demands of the war, men such as John Peak Cushing were in the middle of the fighting. *Scituate's Record of Names* stated that in the Battle of White Oak Swamp, Virginia, John Peak Cushing was wounded June 30, 1862, by a musket ball through his right thigh. The next day, July 1st, he was taken prisoner and carried to Richmond, Virginia. Cushing was paroled on July 27, 1862, in a prisoner exchange between the North and South. He was discharged for disability on November 29, 1862, from Washington, D.C.

On August 4, 1862, President Lincoln issued another Executive Order for 300,000 men, but this time the request was for nine months of service.[17] According to the Commonwealth of Massachusetts General Order No. 58 dated November 22, 1862, included in the Civil War files in the town archives, the state was given a quota of 19,080 to fill. Scituate was expected to supply 47 men. The quotas were listed for neighboring towns: Hingham 88, Hull 5, Marshfield 50, and South Scituate 52.

The pressure for more troops was ever present, and there was talk of a draft to fill the quotas if enough volunteers could not be found. At a Town Meeting held on Friday, the 15th day of August 1862, the voting citizens addressed the latest quota and "voted that the Town pay a bounty of $100 to each volunteer who enlists to fill up the quota of Scituate and being a resident therein under the call of the President of the United States for 300,000 men for 9 months when they shall have been mustered into the service." The town also voted to form a committee of five people to assist the Selectmen in recruiting: Edwin Young, Caleb W. Prouty, Henry Damon, William Ferguson, and Benjamin Brown.

During this time, the town was inundated with General Orders from the Commonwealth of Massachusetts Head-Quarters in Boston, all of which needed immediate attention. If the quota could not be filled quickly, a draft would be instituted. Requests of information were also being sent regularly from the Provost Marshal General's Office in Boston.

COMMONWEALTH OF MASSACHUSETTS.

PROVOST MARSHAL GENERAL'S OFFICE,

BOSTON, December 9th, 1862.

To the Mayors of Cities and the Chairmen of Selectmen of Towns:—

By direction of His Excellency the Governor and Commander-in-Chief, I have the honor to request that you will prepare and return to me a statement setting forth—

1st. The number of men enlisted from your town or city in the three years Regiments, up to the 1st of December current.

2d. The aggregate amount of bounty money paid to them.

3d. The number of men enlisted in the nine months Regiments, up to the 1st of December, current.

4th. The aggregate amount of bounty paid to them.

5th. The aggregate amount of expenses, other than bounties, incurred in the recruiting service, up to the 1st of December, current.

You will please obtain from the private associations in your town or city which have paid bounties to enlisted men, a similar statement, and return it to this office.

It is important that these statistics of the recruiting service should be preserved for the future use of the State. His Excellency desires to lay before the Legislature an exhibit showing the amount which the bounty system has cost the Commonwealth. It will be of great assistance to him if the returns can be furnished on or before the first of January, 1863.

Any statement which you may be able to make concerning the working of the system will also be of service.

Respectfully yours, &c.,

CHARLES F. BLAKE,

Major and Provost Marshal General.

Courtesy of the Scituate Town Archives.

The recruiting committee and the Selectmen recruited 35 Scituate residents to serve for nine months. In order to reach the mandatory town quota of 47, the town of Scituate paid $150 bounty to twelve men from the town of Abington.

Soldier's Letters

As the war continued to keep the soldiers away from home, the men wrote letters to their families in Scituate. Fortunately, some letters written by William Hyland Osborn(e) letters remain today, preserved in a private collection. He was a twenty-year-old shoemaker when he mustered into the 32nd Regiment Massachusetts Volunteer Infantry for three years on December 17, 1861. He was born in Scituate on December 22, 1840, to Caleb and Mary A. Hyland. This letter was written to his mother on May 23, 1862, while the 32nd Regiment Massachusetts was on garrison duty at Fort Warren in Boston Harbor.[18] In the second half of the letter, William described his new uniform and life at Fort Warren:

I saw in the paper that they wanted one hundred thousand more men if that is so we shant stay here all summer.
We have got a new pare of pants and dress coat and a large hat with an egel and bugel and a large fether on it more than all that we shall have bronze scales on our shoulders. I am going to Boston and have my likeness taken with my uniform all on. There is a court marshal here today one of the boys got asleep on his post. I dont know what they will do with him but I gess that they wont shot him that is the law for getting asleep on your post.
I cant think of anything more to write now so good by.

Giv my best Respects to
all that Inquire after me.
Yours Truly
Mr. Wm. H. Osborn
Co. C. First Battalion
The Bloody First
Fort Warren
Boston Harbor
Mass
Pleas do write soon
Good By to all

Courtesy of private collection.

Andrew Murry Hyland, another Scituate soldier, mustered into service on August 20, 1862, for three years in the 38th Regiment Massachusetts Volunteer Infantry. A twenty-one year old shoemaker, Andrew was born in Scituate on April 6, 1841, to parents Peleg and Mary J. His letters are held at the Scituate Historical Society. On September 26, 1862, while in Camp Cram Powhattan, Maryland he wrote a letter to his sister:

Courtesy of the Scituate Historical Society.

dear sister i now take my pen in hand to let you know that i am all well and hope that these few lines will find you the same i got your letter this morning and was glad to hear that you was all smart and i suppose that the baby grows like a good one i am growing fat out here and if i keep on i shall get so fat that is i cant move i weigh 173 pounds now we have every thing that is good to eat henry Brown John Studley and thomas Hayden Bily Bates and Billings Merritt and i are making an oven to bake our beans in. We have to take mud for mortar and a Shingle for a trowel you would laugh to see us at work we work about ten minutes and then rest about an hour or so we are getting Lazy that we hate to go after our diner if we have to Stay here three years we shall be so lazy that we shant never do any thing when we do get home i Suppose that you are drying apples about this time dry up a lot of them so that you can eat some for me We get plenty of peaches here we can get a bushel for fifty cents and good ones to there is a great Battle going on not far from us We can hear them quite plain from Where i am they have ben fighting all day with out stoping and it makes a devil of a racket i wish that we was there to help them we have done some Sham fights so as to get used to it we fire our guns at each other but don't have any thing but powder in it after we have fired we Charge Bayonets in fun when we Charge the Colonel tells

us to hollor like hell that is just the way that he spoke it that is so that we shant hear groans and cries of the wounded it is better fun to try it in fun than it is in ernest I guess and Some times when we Charge Bayonets we drop our guns and make believe fight with our fists and When one gets his cap knocked off he falls down and lays till the fight is over with some times it lasts three and more and it makes us sweat i can tell you i cant think of any thing more to write so good bye and write soon from your brother
Andrew M Hyland

Direct your letters to Powhattan Baltimore County MD Co D 38 reg Mass Vol

tell John Warren that i did not have time to write to him to day but Shall next Sunday if i Can get time if you cant read this you must guess at it i don't have very good accommodations to write so i take it on the ground and lay on my Belly and Write

On October 2, 1862, Hyland wrote a letter to his mother also, from Camp Cram Powhattan.

dear mother i thought that i would write a few lines and let you know that i am well and hope that you are the same i am well and taking comfort i have not got sick of it yet and don't think i shall it grows hot here instead of cool but it is quite cold nights and fogy but about noon it bakes down good every have minute we have to wipe of the sweat we was out on regimental inspection yesterday and it took about three hours to inspect us and the Colonel said that we cept very clean and that our Clothes were kept in good shape to...i have not had a letter from home for more than a week and i want to know why you dont write i have not got any money and i cant write again for i cant get stamps to put on them and i shall expect some money in 4 or 5 days after to day...we had some plum pudding and baked beans for break fast this morning We shall live first rate now that we have got an oven to bake in i cant write any more now so write as soon as you can from your son Andrew M Hyland direct your letters to Powhattan Baltimore County MD Co. D 38 reg Mass vol.

i was reading a Boston paper the other day that said that we had ben in a battle and got cut up Badly But it is not so and you must not Believe any thing that you hear for it wont be true

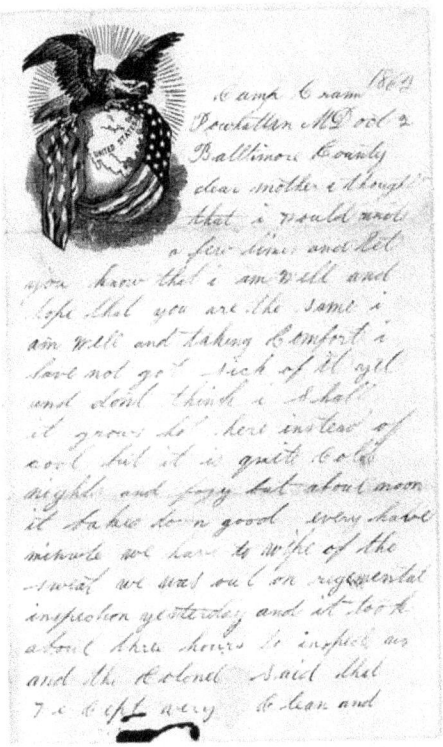

Courtesy of The Scituate Historical Society.

Shortly after writing this letter, Andrew Hyland contracted typhoid fever. On November 17, 1862, he died in Baltimore, Maryland after being sick for two weeks. He had been a soldier for less than three months. He was buried at Loudon National Cemetery in Baltimore.

One of the soldiers to volunteer for nine months was Israel Davis Damon, who mustered into the 43rd Regiment Massachusetts Volunteer Infantry, Company F. Israel was born in Scituate on May 9, 1844, to Israel and Susan (Farrington) and, like his father, worked as a farmer. His letters to his mother are stored and transcribed at the Scituate Historical Society. On November 14, 1862, he wrote this letter while in Beaufort Harbor, North Carolina:

Dear Mother
We finally reached Beufort, having been aboard here over a week, we left Boston about five o'clock monday afternoon and arrived here about twelve today. We have had a rather long voyage. We got aground coming in so we shall have to wait for the night tide before we can get up to the wharf. We came in ahead of the other transports, but we got aground, and they have gone ahead of us. I suppose as soon as we get out of the ship we shall take the cars for Newbern. We had rather a hard time of it in Boston Harbor during the storm but we have had good weather coming out

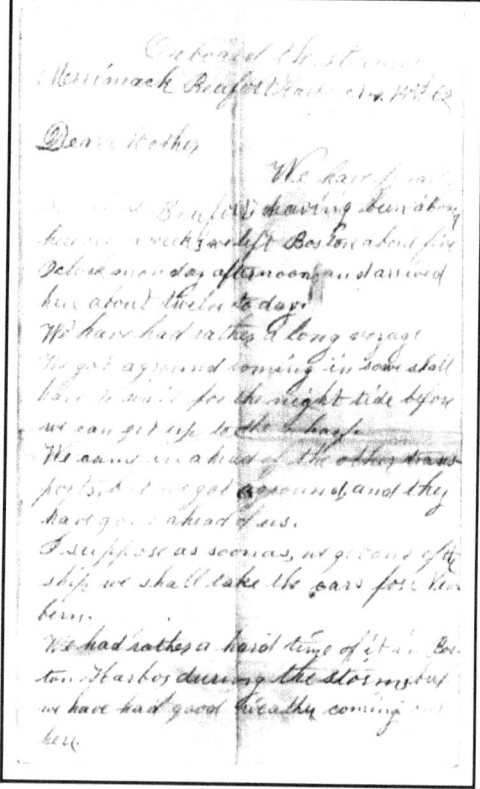

Courtesy of The Scituate Historical Society.

here. There has been considerable seasick here, but I have not been sick. They were rather afraid we should come across the Alabama so they sent a gunboat with us to keep her off. The gunboat could not said very fast so it took us a day or two longer. We were out of sight of land longer than it took then to come the whole distance the other trip. The boys are all well who came from around there. Warren has not been seasick. John says he is all right. Alfred wants you to tell Aunt Elizabeth he is all right only his eyes are pretty sore. I suppose by the time you get this letter we shall be in Newbern. As I cannot think of anything more to write I must bid you goodbye
from your affectionate son
Davis

On the 9th of December the 43rd Regiment Massachusetts received orders to be ready to move. Davis wrote to his mother, "we are to have three days cooked rations and seven days of hard bread and coffee." In a letter dated December 21, 1862, written to his mother, he relayed his experience in the Battle of Kinston in North Carolina.

We started Thursday the 11th a little after 5 O'clock and soon got into Newbern, where we found several other regiments ready to start. We got started about 8 O'clock but for the first two or three hours we did not go more than a mile or two, as there was a kind of sloush in the road which bothered us considerable. As soon as we got over the mud hole we had to march pretty fast till after 1 O'clock. We were nearly melted and tuckered before we came to a halt. They marched so fast that nearly half of our regiment fell out before we halted. We marched about 12 miles that day. We did not march as far as we should have done if the rebels had not blocked up the road. They fell a lot of trees across the road, so we had to stop for the pioneers to clear the road, it took them to nearly midnight to clear the road so that we could get baggage waggons [sic] and artillery along. Our army and baggage train was nearly ten miles long. The second day our cavalry killed two or three *rebels, and took about a dozen prisoners. The rebels burned a small bridge the next day and bothered us for an hour or two. They had a couple of small cannon planted on the other side of the bridge, but our cavalry boys soon drove them off. The cavalry have two small brass pieces with them all the time. They took both the rebel pieces before night. Sunday we came across them near Kingston and the head brigade and three or four regiments of our brigade had quite a tough time of it for three or four hours the 45th got into the thickest of it and suffered considerably, it is said they lost about 60 killed and wounded. The battle lasted about four hours, but our regiment did not get into it. We were so near that once in a while a bullet would whistle pretty near our heads. They couldn't get the rebels in an open field, so they had to fight them in the woods. Our men charged them several times, they drove them every time as the rebels can't stand a bayonet charge very well. The 45th charged on them once and soon scattered them. There was a building in the woods full of rebels where the hardest part of the fighting was, the house was riddled with bullets, and there was hardly a tree what has got bullet marks on it, there are several trees around broken off by our shells. The artillery is what does the business, as the rebels can't stand our shells. Our regiment was stationed on the side of an open field where the Gen thought the rebels would come out if they tried to flank us but they did not try it, so we did not have to fight any...*

Around the same time, the 32nd Regiment Massachusetts Volunteer Infantry was in Virginia. William Hyland Osborn(e) wrote a letter to his father dated 1862 describing the Battle of Fredericksburg on December 11th-14th, 1862, Maj. General Ambrose Burnside had recently replaced Maj. General George McClellan to lead the Army of the Potomac. General Robert E. Lee commanded the Army of Northern Virginia. There were 200,000 troops in the battle that lasted three days.[19] Osborn(e) gave an eyewitness account of the battle:

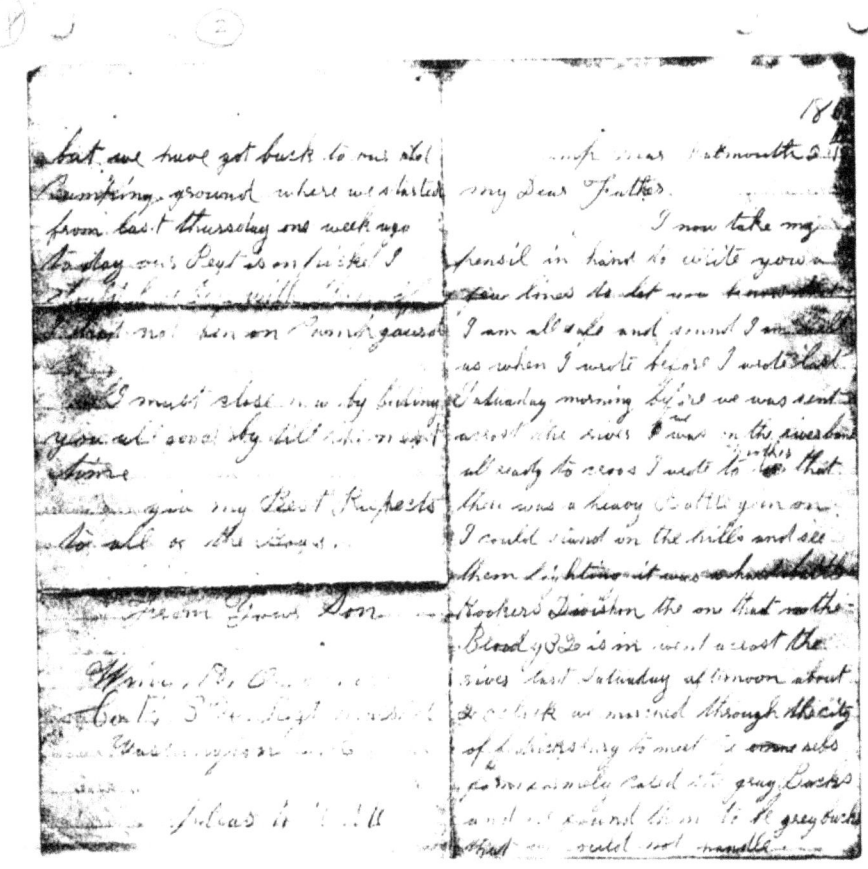

Courtesy of private collection.

1862
Camp near Falmouth
My Dear Father

I now take my pensil in hand to write you a few lines to let you know that I am all safe and sound I am well as when I wrote before I wrote last Saturday morning before we was sent acrost the river we was on the riverbank all ready to cross I wrote to Mother that there was a heavy Battle goin on. I could stand on the hills and see them fighting. It was a hard battle.

Hookers Division the one that the Bloody 32 is in went acrost the river last Saturday afternoon about 2 oclock we marched through the city of fredicksburg to meet the rebs the ones formerly called the gray Backs and we found them to be greybacks that we could not handle.

We marched onto the battle field you can Judge how I felt about that time you nornow[no] one else can have any knowledge of how I felt about them times. of all the growns [groans] and crys that come from the wounded soldiers I thought that I would judge something about it before I went on but I did not know anything about it. when we the 32 went on to the field of battle we went on with our guns loaded and cocked we went in on a charge bayonets the bulets and shell flew like hail stones we lost about 40 kild and wounded 3 or 4 kild several more missing that we dont know any thing about where they are but these 40 we know there they are but thank god I did not get a scratch on me but it looked dark I can tell you for a spell. when we went on to the field Saturday afternoon we left we layed all night Saturday all day Sunday till night without our blanket the dead and wounded layed on the field that night and when we come of[f] from the field for we had as much as we could do to get of[f] our selfs I could write all over 3 sheets of paper like this but I must clowse [close] by saying one thing that the soldiers will never fight again again under Burnside he is not the man for that place. In this last battle we have lost over 40,000 med kiled and wounded some say that there was not so many but I hedr our Colonel say that it would come nearer that then any thing else.
give us General McCellen and we will follow him any where he is [assigned] to go but not Old Burnside. The soldiers are down on him for leading us into such a place but we have got back to our old camping ground where we started from last thursday one week ago today our Regt is on picket I thought I would have ben with them if I had not ben on Camp guard

I must close now by bidding you all good by till the next time
Give my Best Respects to all of the Boys
From Your Son
Wim. H. Osborn
Co E 32 Regt Mass Vol
Washington DC

Pleas do Write

CHAPTER 6

1863: CALLS FOR SOLDIERS AND THE DRAFT

On January 1, 1863, President Abraham Lincoln signed the Emancipation Proclamation that he had issued one hundred days earlier on September 22, 1862, shortly after the battle of Antietam. President Lincoln stated that:

> By virtue of the power, and for the purpose aforesaid, I do order and declare that all persons held as slaves within said designated States, and parts of States, are, and hence-forward shall be free; and that the Executive government of the United States, including the military and naval authorities thereof, will recognize and maintain the freedom of said persons.[20]

Town Reports for Year Ending February 28, 1863

As the war continued, the selectmen primarily focused on the overwhelming tasks associated with the war. In the *Report of the Selectmen on the Financial Affairs of the Town of Scituate, for*

Year Ending Feb 28, 1863, the financial statements included ordinary expenses of $1,841.89 for schools, $942.97 for the poor, $318.75 for town officers, $61.72 for roads and bridges, and $85.05 for the repair of public buildings. The ongoing war imposed additional expenses. In this annual report the Selectmen George E. Cole and George C. Lee explained "the past year having been exceptional in the character of its expenditures, we have prepared the following Statement, distinguishing the ordinary from the extraordinary expenditures." The extraordinary expense included $8,000.00 for bounties and $211.72 for enrolling, recruiting, and exempting soldiers. The selectmen also provided this disclosure:

> The unusual demands upon the time of the selectmen during the past year have prevented such an examination of localities as would be necessary to make a detailed report upon the subject of Guide Boards…in view of the fact that nearly one hundred families in town have a special interest in military matters, and all a general interest, we venture to lengthen the Report by annexing to its statements in detail of all the Military Expenditures, together with the names of the Volunteers in the Army from Scituate.

The town reported a total number of 128 volunteers from Scituate as of February 19, 1863. In the list of soldiers that volunteered, there were three soldiers that had the word "deceased" written next to their name: Charles Henry Clapp, Seth Bailey, and George D. Brown. Charles Henry Clapp, a stagecoach driver, son of Charles and Anna, died February 21, 1863, in a camp near Falmouth, Virginia of congestion of the lungs. Seth K. Bailey, a carpenter, son of Amasa and Sally (Kent) Bailey, died at a camp in Baltimore, Maryland on September 6, 1862. George D. Brown, a nail cutter, son of John and Clarissa (Cook) Bailey was killed on June 15, 1862, while on picket duty at Fair Oaks, Virginia.

As citizens left to serve in the military, town positions became vacant until a replacement could be found. For example, the *Report of the School Committee* of that year noted that "the school at Town Hall was suspended for four weeks last Autumn, by the teacher's enlisting for military service, and by the going away of one of the School committee for the same purpose, and another to help in a Soldiers' Hospital."

It is important to note that Scituate was determined to make education a priority even in the midst of war. The following statement appeared in the 1863 *Report of the School Committee*:

> The School Committee, in common with all the citizens, are in favor of economy, and or retrenchment, too, whenever practicable; but they trust that nothing but poverty, or war in our own borders, will lower our appropriations or interrupt the keeping of any of our eleven schools, or cut down the fair wages for teaching. The value of real estate and the attractions of a town are enhanced by good schools; and it reflects great honor upon Scituate, that she sustains a High School nine months of the year, though not obliged by the number of inhabitants to do so.

At this 1863 annual town meeting, George C. Lee, Roland Turner and Thomas Vinal were voted as selectmen for the next year, entrusted by their community to oversee Scituate during this national crisis.

William H. Osborn(e) Letter

On May 31, 1863, William H Osborn(e) wrote a letter to his mother. In the letter he described trading with Confederate soldiers across a river.

On picket kempers ford Va
May 31st 1863
My Dear Mother,
    It is with pleasure that I sit down to write you a few lines to informe you that I am well as when I wrote home before and hope that this will find you all well at home as for the news there is not much to write. I wrote home in my last leter that we was doing guard duty at Stonemans Switch but now we are 18 miles from there. My [illegible] is guarding the fords from falmouth up the river. my Brigade is guarding three fords the 9 mass is at barneys ford. the 32 is at kempers ford the 62 P.V. is at kelley ford with the michigan the ford here we are is not but about 4 rods wide the water is up to my midle the rebs are on one side of the ford and we are the other all in site we sit on one side of the river and the gray backs on the other and talk to one other one of our boys asked them if they would like to have some coffe they said yes so one of there made a boat out of a piece of bark and send it acros the river with a tin box tied one to it and we sent enough for to cups of coffee. they was glad to get it they wanted one of us to come over where they was we told them that we could not see that then one of them said that he was coming over last night we told him to come along but we have not seen him yet. I gess he did not get a chance...

A few days later on July 2, 1863, Osborn(e) was wounded at the Battle of Gettysburg, Pennsylvania. *Scituate's Book of Records* recorded that he was hit "in the knee by a fragment of a Shell." He survived the war, mustering out of U. S. Service on December 16, 1864.

William H. Whipple, 54th Regiment Mass. Volunteer Infantry

On January 20, 1863, the Federal Government authorized Governor Andrew to form a black regiment, and the Governor appointed Robert Gould Shaw to command the new regiment.

This 54th Regiment Massachusetts Volunteer Infantry fought on the front lines of the mission to capture Fort Wagner in South Carolina. In the evening of July 18, 1863, the regiment was overrun by Confederate soldiers. The death toll of the regiment was devastating.

William Henry Whipple, a twenty-one year old waiter and resident of Scituate, served in the 54th Regiment Massachusetts Volunteer Infantry. Whipple was listed as part of the town's quota in the Town Report year ending March 3, 1864, but not in *Scituate's Record of Names*. He had enlisted May 5, 1863, and mustered into service on May 12, 1863. The *Massachusetts Soldiers, Sailors and Marines in the Civil War* states that he was wounded July 18, 1863, at Fort Wagner, South Carolina, and was discharged February 24, 1864, for wounds.[21]

The Draft

In the summer of 1863, the federal government instituted a draft. Those drafted had the option to pay a commutation fee of $300 to the United States Government, or to find a substitute to serve the time. In response to the draft, riots broke out in New York City, as well as in Boston in July. Howard T. Oedel noted in *Massachusetts in the Civil War Volume IV A Year of Dedication 1863-1864* that:

> During June and July all men 20 to 45 years of age were enrolled for the draft. The total number of Massachusetts came to 164,178. Of this number, 32,079 were drawn, of which 22,343 obtained exemptions and 3,046 failed to report. Of the number drafted 6,690 were obligated to serve. Of these 743 offered to serve personally and 2,325 more procured substitutes, while 3,623 others paid the government a total of $1,085,800 to avoid military service.[22]

The Report of the Selectmen on the Financial Affairs of The Town of Scituate, for Year Ending March 3, 1864, confirmed that three men had been drafted from Scituate on July 20, 1863: Ashael F. Nott, Luke G. Fitts, and John Tirrell.

Ashael Nott, married, age 33, shoemaker, had already served, mustering in the 7th Regiment Mass. Volunteer Infantry on June 15, 1861, and had been discharged on December 3, 1862, for disability. Seven months later his name was pulled for the draft, and he served again, this time in the 32nd Regiment Mass. Volunteer Infantry, Company E for three years. He was wounded in the arm on May 7, 1864, at Wilderness, Virginia and mustered out of service July 12, 1865.

James Tirrell, a farmer in Scituate, was drafted into the 32nd Regiment, Company E for three years. He was killed at Petersburg, Virginia on June 18, 1864.

Luke Fitts, married, age 32, shoemaker, was also assigned to the 32nd Regiment, Company E. On May 12, 1864, he was wounded by a musket ball through the left hand at Laurel Hill, Virginia and discharged for wounds on October 25, 1864.

Call for 300,000 Volunteers October 17, 1863

In spite of the volunteers and draft, the war demanded more men. As a result, on October 17, 1863, President Lincoln called for additional troops. Issued from the Commonwealth of Massachusetts Head Quarters [sic] in Boston on October 29, 1863, General Order No. 30 is included in the Civil War files in the town archives. The first few paragraphs describe the continued pressure on Massachusetts to fill the quotas.

> The President of the United States, under date of October 17, 1863, has issued a call for 300,000 volunteers, to serve for three years or the War, but not exceeding three years; and the quota assigned to Massachusetts under this call, amounts to 15,126. If this number is not raised by voluntary enlistment, a draft will be ordered to supply the deficiency, which draft will commence on the fifth day of January next.
>
> The time for action is short, and the greatest activity and promptitude will be necessary, to fulfill the demand of the Government, before the time prescribed for commencing the draft. The Mayor and Alderman of Cities, and the Selectmen of Towns, are again urgently requested to use their official and personal influence, and obtain the energetic co-operation of all those whose hearts are in the work, to furnish their proportions of volunteers; to call public meetings, and adopt other efficient measurers, to draw forth and stimulate the public interest in the cause.

As part of District No. 2, Scituate needed to find another 28 men to serve. The neighboring towns received their quotas too: South Scituate 21, Marshfield 19, Cohasset 24, Hull 4, Hingham 50, Abington 91.

On November 30, 1863, a recruiting office was established at Town Hall in Scituate. It was opened every day except Sunday from 8:30am to 12:00pm and from 1:00pm to 4:00pm. The recruiting officers were George C. Lee, Thomas Vinal, and Roland Turner.

CHAPTER 7

1864: SCITUATE SAILORS AND FILLING QUOTA

The year of 1864 opened with another request for volunteers. On February 1, 1864, the President ordered a call for an additional 200,000 troops. Massachusetts was responsible for providing 22,000 men.[23] Scituate was given a quota of 25 men. A letter dated February 10, 1864, from J.W.D. Hall, Provost Marshal of the Second District in Taunton, Massachusetts, requested quota information from the town.

Provost Marshal's Office,
Second District, Mass.

Taunton, Feb. 10th, 1864

Chairman of Recruiting Committee:—
DEAR SIR—

Will you please to inform me whether the quota of your town, under the recent call for 300,000 men, is filled? If not, how many have you recruited? And what is the prospect for completing your quota by March first?

Also, whether your quota, under the last call, for 200,000 men will be filled by the first of March?

Preparations for the contemplated draft on the 10th of March are nearly completed, and an immediate answer to these questions is respectfully solicited by

Yours, Respectfully,
J. W. D. HALL,
Provost Marshal,
2d Dist. Mass.

Courtesy of The Scituate Town Archives.

The selectmen of Scituate received a handwritten letter from Hall dated March 2, 1864. The reference in the letter to the call of 500,000 and Scituate's quota of 53 men combines the call for 300,000 men on October 17, 1863, (28 men) and the call for 200,000 on February 1, 1864, (25 men).

Courtesy of The Scituate Town Archives.

Geo. C. Lee Esq.
>Selectmen of Scituate.
>Dr Sir
>>Yours of the 29th duly received. The quota of Scituate made under the call for 500,000 men is 53.
>Deducting the product of the draft, -all who paid commutation, furnished substitutes, and rendered personal service- 17, will leave 36 to be filled by recruiting by draft now ordered. The 36 men must be "mustered into service", or they will not be counted. Hoping you have accomplished your purpose
>>I am respectfully Yours,
>>J.W.D. Hall Pro Marshall
>>2d Dist. Mass.

Another source documented events that took place in Scituate during this time. The February 26, 1864, edition of *The Hingham Journal and South Shore Advertiser* (Vol. 15 No. 9) printed a small article about a local military parade and fundraiser:

> Military Parade.
> The 22d of February at Scituate was celebrated by a parade of the 5th Company "State Guard" under the command of Capt. C.W. Prouty, (who turned out with 64 muskets,) in uniform. The uniform is blue coats and pants, with the State buttons, and Kossuth hats, having on the front "S.G." and figure 5. The Company was organized on the 10th November last. The number enrolled is 111. The town has fitted up an armory at the expense of $250, in Union Hall building. The State has furnished the Company with 96 muskets and buff leather equipments. This being their first public appearance, it was said they made a fine show, considering the time since their organization. A collation was served in their armory during the day. In the evening, the Ladies Soldiers' Aid Society gave an entertainment at Union Hall, for the

purpose of raising funds. The hall was filled to overflowing, and many were refused admission, owing to every setting and standing place being filled. The arrangements for the day and evening were a complete success. The officers of the Guards were as follows: C.W. Prouty, Captain; Joseph Northey, 1st Lieut.; Joseph W. Tilden, 2d Lieut.; B. Brown, I.O. Cole, R. Clapp, Jao. Cushing, and Wm. Young, Sergeants; R. Cook, H. Clapp, J. Manson, Issac Litchfield, [illegible] Sylvester, [illegible] Gardner, W.J. Newcomb, and I. Litchfield, Corporals; Rev. A. I. Sessions and Rev. W. G. Babcock, Chaplains. About four-fifths of the members are over 45 years of age.

On March 14, 1864, the federal government made yet another call for 200,000 men to serve, requiring 22,000 men from Massachusetts.[24] A young man from Scituate, George Whitmarsh Perry born December 15, 1846, to Samuel N. and Eliza (Bryant) Perry and worked as a farmer and shoemaker volunteered under this latest call for soldiers. He had already served his country earlier in the war, enlisting at the age of sixteen on September 2, 1862, for nine months in the 43rd Regiment Mass. Volunteer Infantry, Company F. On March 17, 1864, he enlisted again as a private in the 58th Regiment Mass. Volunteer Infantry, Company I. He was promoted to sergeant. Perry was taken prisoner of war on September 30, 1864, in Virginia. On January 13, 1865, he died of disease at Salisbury prison in North Carolina. The local chapter of the Civil War veterans' organization, The Grand Army of the Republic Post No. 31 in Scituate, was named in his honor, to forever remember their fellow soldier, neighbor, and friend.

The Scituate Ladies Sanitary Association 1864

The Scituate Ladies Sanitary Association continued to meet. On May 10, 1864, the minutes reported that "the following articles were sent to Massachusetts Military agent in Washington D.C.: 54 pairs socks, 5 quilts, 17 shirts, 10 pair drawers, 4 dressing gowns, 6 towels, 1 table cloth, 5 handkerchiefs and large bundle of pamphlets and papers." On June 24, 1864, another shipment contained "a box of hospital supplies containing 54 handkerchiefs, 4 quilts, 5 shirts, 2 sheets, rags, a gallon of Elderberry wine, 2 jars raspberry jams, papers and pamphlets."

Mrs. Clara Turner Bates, one of the officers, worked to support and improve the conditions of all soldiers, but she could not save her son, Charles Eugene. He enlisted August 11, 1862, in the 39th Regiment Mass. Volunteer Infantry, Company G. Charles was wounded in the left arm on May 8, 1864, at Laurel Hill, Virginia. On November 2, 1864, he died at Jarvis Hospital in Baltimore, Maryland of diptheria after being sick for eight days.

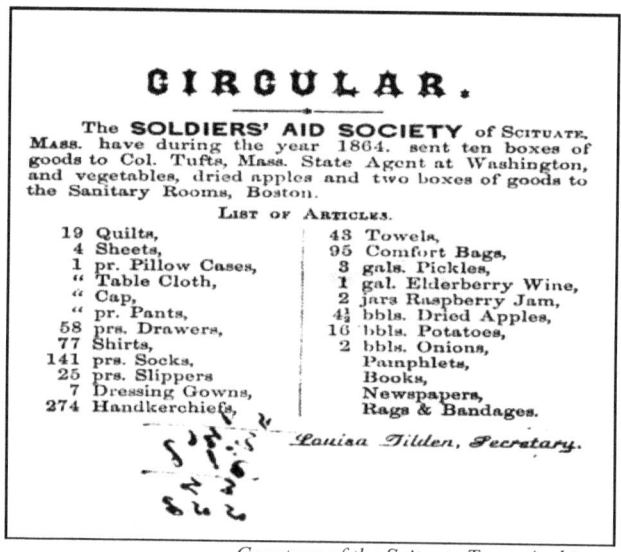

Courtesy of the Scituate Town Archives.

Scituate Sailors in the Civil War

Since the start of the war, men from Scituate had volunteered to serve in the Navy. According to the Federal Government, however, their service was not considered part of the quota for the town or the state. In 1864 Governor Andrew finally received federal permission to include men serving in the naval service as part of the state's quota, which took a little pressure off Scituate and the state.[25]

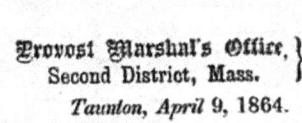

Provost Marshal's Office,
Second District, Mass.
Taunton, April 9, 1864.

SIR :—

Agreeably to instructions from the Provost Marshal General, received this day, the Chairman of the Board of Selectmen of each town is requested to send to this Office a list of those who have enlisted in the Navy previous to the 24th of February, 1864, giving age, occupation, place where enlisted, the name of the vessel in which each man went to sea, and the Sub-District of which he is a citizen—the latter fact to be established by the sworn affidavit of the aforesaid Chairman.

You are hereby requested to comply with these instructions that your town may be duly credited with all persons in the naval service, agreeably to the law of Feb. 24th, 1864. Annexed is a form for your guidance.

Respectfully Yours,
J. W. D. HALL,
Provost Marshal, 2d Dist. Mass.

Courtesy of the Scituate Town Archives.

The *Report of the Selectmen on the Financial Affairs of the Town of Scituate, for the Year Ending March 5, 1865,* listed seven seamen that were claimed and allowed in the quota of Scituate at this time. The *Massachusetts Soldiers, Sailors, and Marines in the Civil War, Volume VII* confirmed that the men were credited to Scituate: John Barrows, George Sherman Bates, George Nelson Bramhall, Thomas M. Burnett, William Thomas Burrows (Burroughs), Francis Marion Cook, and Ethan Allen Stetson Pool.

Finding Recruits in Boston

After three years of war, a significant number of men ages 18 to 45 were serving or had already served in the war and even though men from Scituate continued to enlist, more recruits were needed. The quota must be filled. A resident of Scituate and a former Town Clerk, J. O. Cole was given the task of securing volunteers to satisfy Scituate's quota. This included going to Boston to pursue options with brokers, who had established offices that offered to find recruits to fill town quotas. The town records show that the amount paid for each bounty increased during this time, and an additional bounty was paid by an unnamed private source, most likely a group of local citizens able to financially assist the town. A series of letters written in 1864 by J. O. Cole to Scituate Selectman G. C. Lee was found in the town archive's Civil War files.

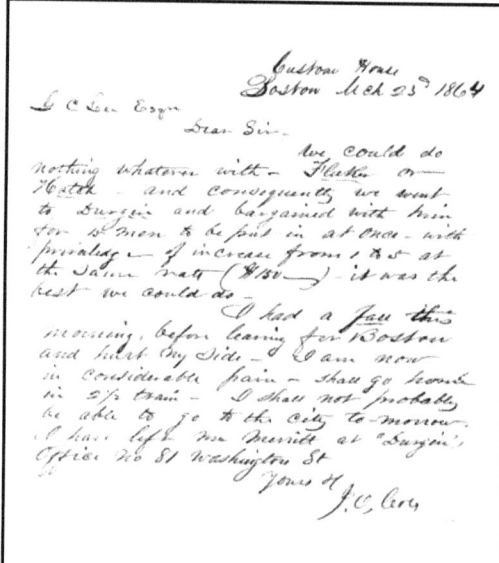

Courtesy of the Scituate Town Archives.

Custom House
Boston Mch 23d 1864
G C Lee Esq
Dear Sir-
We could do nothing whatever with – <u>Fluker</u> or <u>Hatch</u> – and consequently we went to <u>Durgin</u> and bargained for 15 men to be put in at once – with privilege of increase from 1 to 5 at the same rate ($150-) it was the best we could do-

    I had a <u>fall</u> this morning, before leaving for Boston and hurt my side – I am now in considerable pain – shall go home in 2 ½ train – I shall not probably be able to go to the city to-morrow. I have left Mr. Merritt at "Durgin" Office No 81 Washington St.
Yours
J. O. Cole

Custom House
Boston June 29, 64
G C Lee Esq
Dear Sir
I have made some inquiries with regard to getting recruits and I find that $300 is the present price. I do not think it is advisable to undertake to procure any at present but wait awhile till the present call is satisfied then there will be less anxiety for the future - I Have no doubt but that there will be a call for more troops by the 10th July – but you will see by the papers that the act that has passed the House (which I think will be substantially the law that will pass/ repeals the commutation clause but the other provisions more than compensate in my opinion – You will see we shall be given 60 Days to volunteer after the call is made & we can do that for 1, 2, & 3 years and receive 1, 2, or 3 hundred dollars bounty and also you will see that the executive of the State has a right to go into any insurgent State and procure recruits – Now I think that all of these considerations will tend to bring the price of men down to our means-
truly yours
J.O. Cole

July 18, 1864 Proclamation Calling for 500,000 Volunteers

President Abraham Lincoln issued Proclamation 116 on July 18, 1864, in order to

> Call for 500,000 volunteers for the military service, Provided, nevertheless, that this call shall be reduced by all credits which may be established under section 8 of the aforesaid act on account of persons who have entered the naval service during the present rebellion and by credits for men furnished to the military service in excess of calls heretofore made. Volunteers will be accepted under this call for one, two, or three years, as they may elect, and will be entitled to the bounty provided by the law for the period of service for which they enlist.[26]

The town of Scituate was expected to enlist 45 men to fulfill this quota. A few days later a petition from citizens of Scituate dated July 22, 1864, was sent to the Selectmen.

To the Selectmen of the town of Scituate
We, the undersigned inhabitants, legal voters of the Town of Scituate, respectfully request your Honorable Board, to call a meeting of the inhabitants of said town, qualified to vote in town affairs, on Saturday the 30th inst., or as soon hereafter as it may legally be done, for the following purposes: First to Choose a Moderator Second To know what action the Town will take towards carrying out the vote of the Town, passed in May 1861, promising allowances and extra pay to soldiers then volunteering during the time they were in the service of the United States, and act or do anything relative to the above.

> Scituate, July 22d 1864,
> To the Selectmen of the Town of Scituate
> We, the undersigned inhabitants & legal Voters
> of the Town of Scituate, respectfully request your Honor-
> -able Board, to call a meeting of the inhabitants
> of said town, qualified to vote in town affairs,
> on Saturday the 30th inst, or as soon hereafter
> as it may legally be done, for the following purposes.
> To Wit: First, to Choose a Moderator —
> Second — To know what action the Town
> will take towards carrying out the vote of the
> Town, passed in May 1861, promising allowances
> and extra pay to Soldiers then volunteering, during
> the time they were in the Service of the United
> States, and act or do any thing relative to the above —
>
> Names.   Names.
> Edward James   Fredric Sanborn
> ...   ... Young
> Daniel ...
> Benjamin Totman
> Charles O. Ellms
> Samuel J. Hurst
> William H. Totman
> William Litchfield
> Galen Litchfield
> G. Y. Sylvester

Courtesy of the Scituate Town Archives.

Twelve signatures listed on the paper include Edward James, Charles O. Ellms, William Totman, William Litchfield, Galen Litchfield and G. Y. Sylvester.

The 1864 Presidential Election

On Tuesday, the 8th day of November 1864 the Scituate residents qualified to vote met at Town Hall and cast their votes for the President and Vice President of the United States and for state and county offices. Abraham Lincoln and Andrew Johnson, representing the Republic Party, received 314 votes, and George McClellan and George Pendleton, nominated by the Democrats, received 132 votes.

Contraband included in Scituate's Quota of 1864

In the *Report of the Selectmen on the Financial Affairs of the Town of Scituate, for Year Ending March 5, 1865*, and in *The Record of Names*, four volunteers are listed as contrabands from Vicksburg, Mississippi: Moses Sweatman, Clairborne Downs, Michael Johnson, and George W. Bass. Scituate paid a bounty of $125 for each of the soldiers. The term contraband during this time often referred to freed slaves. Research has revealed that the men had been recruited by Northern states to serve in the Union Army, a practice that had been approved by an Act of Congress on July 4, 1864. Because towns and cities were struggling to meet yet another quota, Massachusetts took the opportunity to enlist men from Southern states that could be credited to Massachusetts. A Board of Recruitment from the Massachusetts oversaw the appropriation and crediting to the towns and cities.[34]

While the background of the men was not known, they are documented in the *Massachusetts Soldiers, Sailors and Marines in the Civil War*. The section, "Mass. Soldiers in United States Colored Troops of Volume VII" included Clairborne Downs, a 20-year-old laborer that enlisted on October 11, 1864, at Vicksburg, Mississippi for three years and mustered into service October 17, 1864, as a private in Company K of the 5th Colored Heavy Artillery. He mustered out on May 20, 1866.[28] Moses Sweatman was an 18-year-old farmer that enlisted on December 20, 1864, at Vicksburg, Mississippi for three years and mustered into service on December 22, 1864, as a Private in Company E of the 5th Colored Heavy Artillery. He died of disease on July 18, 1865.[29]

The other two men were contraband enlistees who had served in the military organizations from other states. Michael Johnson, a

19-year-old laborer, enlisted on August 31, 1864, for three years and served as a private in the 72nd Illinois Volunteer Infantry.[30] George W. Bass, a 39-year-old machinist enlisted August 20, 1864, and served in the 1st Louisiana Calvary; he mustered out of service on September 11, 1865.[31]

CHAPTER 8

1865: THE CIVIL WAR ENDS

At the inauguration to his second term on March 4, 1865, President Lincoln spoke of the end of the war:

> With malice toward none; with charity for all; with firmness in the right, as God gives us to see the right, let us strive on to finish the work we are in; to bind up the nation's wounds; to care for him who shall have borne the battle, and for his widow, and his orphan-to do all which may achieve and cherish a just, and a lasting peace, among ourselves, and with all nations.[32]

On April 7, 1865, a poem submitted by a resident of North Scituate appeared on the front page of the *Hingham Journal and South Shore Advertiser* (Vol. 16 No. 14).

The Soldier's Death

Far away from the home where his loved ones dwell,
The Soldier sank to rest;
Where no mother's tears o'er his pillow fell,
No kiss on his brow was pres't,
No brother was near to clasp his hand,
No sister his eyes to close;
But far away in a stranger land,
He sank to his last repose.

Strangers were gathered around his bed,
Till his life's last sands were spent,
And as his ransomed spirit fled,
O'er him in prayer they bent.
And when the muffled drums were heard,
Full many an eye grew dim,
For hearts, by kindred ties unstirred,
Mourned earnestly for him.

And oh! how sad these hearts at home,
Following him in prayer;
Continuing the days ere he should come
To fill his vacant chair.
How fearfully those hearts were tried,
What need of Christian trust,
When 'stead of him their hope and pride,
They welcome but his dust!

North Scituate

On April 9, 1865, in a field in the town of Appomattox Court House, Virginia, a white flag was raised, turning the country toward peace, but not soon enough to spare the lives of over six hundred thousand men, or prevent the tremendous pain and suffering of the soldiers and their families.

As peace became a reality, John Wilkes Booth shot President Lincoln on April 14, 1865, at the Ford's Theatre in Washington, D.C. Lincoln died on April 15, 1865. Along with the shock of losing the President, families throughout the country had to carry on without their lost sons, brothers, and husbands. With the war at its end, the surviving soldiers slowly made their way back home. Many of Scituate's soldiers were not discharged until the summer. An article in the *Hingham Journal and South Shore Advertiser* on Friday May 12, 1865, (Vol. 16 No. 19) encouraged support for the returning soldiers.

> The Union Army. The great volunteer army of the Union is in the process of disruption. All over the land,- in the hospitals, at the recruiting rendezvous, and in the camps-soldiers are receiving honorable discharges from the service in which they have done such noble and effective work. We suppose the month of May will not have passed before our army will be reduced to one-quarter of the strength at which it has been maintained during the last three years. It is an immense work that this American Volunteer Army has achieved. Immense suffering they have borne; sublime heroism they have exhibited. Immortal honors they have won, They return to their homes with the grand consciousness that they have effected their work, that they have crushed the rebellion, saved the Union, and won for themselves and for us, a country. The army will be resolved into the great Body of the citizens of the republic. The men who left their farms, their workshops, their stores and their offices to don the army blue and shoulder the musket, will now doff their military costume and return to the peaceful

evolution of civil life. We welcome home our brave soldiers. Let their country receive them with pride and gratitude, and let every one do all his power to give them place and practical aid in the pursuits and professions which they may desire to enter.

This desire to commemorate the heroism of Scituate's veterans appears in the *School Committee Report for year ending March 4, 1866*, when Superintendent G. Hubert Bates wrote that:

An effort had been made to impress upon the minds of the children the great events of the times, together with the love of country, and some of its recent history. On the Fourth of July, the schools joined in a reception of soldiers, and a celebration of the return of peace. They had been represented in the army of the Union by a noble little band, some of whom are numbered with the fallen; and, while we twine around their precious memories the unfading laurel, we render thanksgiving for the triumph of their cause...

One of the last entries in the Ladies Sanitary Association of Scituate dated Sept 26, 1865:

Voted to give the following sums to five Sick Soldiers viz Five dollars to Sumner Litchfield five dollars to Billings Merritt, five dollars to Davis Witherell, five dollars to Melzar Ellms, and the balance, (twenty four) dollars to John Cushing. Voted that Mrs. C. Bates, J.W. Morris and L. Tilden a Committee to carry out the above vote.
Voted the records be placed with the town books.
Adjourned Sini Dim
L. Tilden Secy.

> Voted to give the following sums to five sick Soldiers viz Five dollars to Sumner Litchfield five dollars to Billings Merritt, five dollars to Davis Wetherell, five dollars to Melzar Ellms, and the balance, (twenty four dollars) to John Cushing
> Voted, that Mrs C. Bates. J. W. Morris + L. Tilden a committee to carry out the above vote.
> Voted the records be placed with the towns books
> Adjourned Sine Dine
>   L. Tilden Secy

Courtesy of The Scituate Town Archives.

John Peak Cushing was the first citizen listed in *Scituate's Record of Names* enlisting on April 16, 1861, the day after President Lincoln made that first call for 75,000 volunteers. He mustered out August 1, 1861, completing his three-month service only to volunteer again weeks later for three years. On September 26, 1865, John Peak Cushing was the last soldier listed in the minutes of the Scituate Ladies Sanitary Association. He survived the war, but by voting to give him the bulk of the funds, his neighbors and friends recognized that he was suffering and in great need. Fortunately, a happier time was also documented. The town records show that John Peak Cushing married Martha Ann Seaverns in Scituate on December 24, 1868.

The Civil War swept the people of Scituate, as well as the entire country, into a struggle for survival. The relentless quotas for more men to serve reached deep into the population of small towns. The selectmen of Scituate had the challenge to fill the mandated quotas, while also personally knowing most of the men and their families that volunteered to fight to preserve the United States of America. It was clear in the town documents that as the men stepped forward to serve, the citizens of Scituate also stepped forward determined to take care of their soldiers and each other. Not long after the war, the local veterans established the George W. Perry Post No. 31 of The Grand Army of the Republic. It took a few more years for a memorial to be built to the soldiers and sailors, but both still stand today to honor and remember those that served in America's Civil War.

Notes

1. Roy P. Basler, *Abraham Lincoln speeches and writings 1859-1865* (New York: The Library of America, 1989), 232.
2. Samuel Deane, *History of Scituate, Massachusetts from its First Settlements to 1831* (Boston: James Loring, 1831), 8.
3. Vernon L. Briggs, *History of Shipbuilding on the North River, Plymouth County, MA* (Boston: Coburn Brothers Printers, 1899), 393-407.
4. Barbara Murphy, *Irish Mossers and Scituate Harbour Village* (1980), 21-26.
5. *Old Scituate* (Chief Justice chapter Daughters of the American Revolution, 1921), 65.
6. Harvey Hunter Pratt, *The Early Planters of Scituate a History of the Town of Scituate, Massachusetts from its Establishment to the end of the Revolutionary War*(Published by the Scituate Historical Society, 1929), 272-275.
7. W.G.B., "Extract of a Letter," *The Liberator*, January 4, 1861.
8. Roy P. Basler, *Abraham Lincoln speeches and writings 1859-1865* (New York: The Library of America, 1989), 223-224.
9. Civil War Facts. National Park Service U.S. Department of the Interior, last

modified February 27, 2015, accessed March 10, 2015, http://www.nps.gov/civilwar/facts.htm.

10. Abraham Lincoln: "Proclamation 83 – Increasing the Size of the Army and Navy", May 3, 1861. Online by Gerhard Peters and John T. Woolley, *The American Presidency Project*, accessed March 24, 2015, http://www.presidency.ucsb.edu/ws/?pid=70123.

11. Jordan D. Fiore, *Massachusetts in the Civil War Volume II The Year of Trial and Testing 1861-1862* (Boston: Massachusetts Civil War Centennial Commission, 1961),

12. Gerald Post, *First Guide to Civil War Genealogy and Research 3rd Edition* (Bloomington, Indiana: Trafford, 2010), 23.

13. Letter to Countrywomen from U.S. Sanitary commission. Treasury Building, Washington dated October 1, 1861 from Winfield Scott, Washington September 30, 1861.

14. *Old Scituate* (Chief Justice chapter Daughters of the American Revolution, 1921), 114-115.

15. Abraham Lincoln: "Executive Order," July 1, 1862. Online by Gerhard Peters and John T. Woolley, *The American Presidency Project*, accessed March 24, 2015, http://www.presidency.ucsb.edu/ws/?pid=69811.

16. Edward W. Ellsworth, *Massachusetts in the Civil War Volume III A Year of Crisis 1862-1863* (Boston: Massachusetts Civil War Centennial Commission, 1962), 10.

17. Abraham Lincoln: "Executive Order," August 4, 1862. Online by Gerhard Peters and John T. Woolley, *The American Presidency Project*, accessed March 26, 2015, http://www.presidency.ucsb.edu/ws/?pid=69818.

18. *Massachusetts Soldiers, Sailors, and Marines in the Civil War Vol. III*, compiled and published by The Adjutant General (Norwood, Massachusetts: Norwood Press, 1932), 448.

19. Geoffrey C. Ward with Ric Burns and Ken Burns, *The Civil War an Illustrated History* (New York: Alfred A. Knopf, 1990), 167-174.

20. Roy P. Basler, *Abraham Lincoln Speeches and Writings 1859-1865* (New York: The Library of America, 1989), 425.

21. *Massachusetts Soldiers, Sailors, and Marines in the Civil War Vol. IV*, compiled and published by The Adjutant General (Norwood, Massachusetts: Norwood Press, 1932), 664.

22. Howard T. Oedel, *Massachusetts in the Civil War Volume IV A Year of Dedication 1863-1864* (Boston: Massachusetts Civil War Centennial Commission, 1961), 14.

23. Ibid., 24.

24. Ibid., 24.

25. Ibid., 15.

26. Roy P. Basler, *Abraham Lincoln Speeches and Writings 1859-1865* (New York: The Library of America, 1989), 610.

27. *Massachusetts Soldiers, Sailors, and Marines in the Civil War Vol. VII*, compiled and published by The Adjutant General (Norwood, Massachusetts: Norwood Press, 1933), 316.

28. Ibid., 341.

29. Ibid., 400.

30. *Massachusetts Soldiers, Sailors, and Marines in the Civil War Vol. VI*, compiled and published by The Adjutant General (Norwood, Massachusetts: Norwood Press, 1933), 721.

31. *Massachusetts Soldiers, Sailors, and Marines in the Civil War Vol. VI*, compiled and published by The Adjutant General (Norwood, Massachusetts: Norwood Press, 1933), 726.

32. Roy P. Basler, *Abraham Lincoln Speeches and Writings 1859-1865* (New York: The Library of America, 1989), 687.

Part II

The Grand Army of the Republic, George W. Perry Post No. 31
By Florence Mehegan Ely

The Civil War, the War Between the States, the War of Rebellion - whatever name is used for the conflict that raged on American soil from 1861 to 1865, left scars upon the country that are still evident today. Just as in every war, those that joined up voluntarily or were conscripted, whether they returned whole or disabled, and the families of those who died, paid the greatest price. How could their contributions and sacrifice be recognized? And how could the camaraderie that kept them together in battle be harnessed as a positive force in civilian life?

One veteran, an infantry surgeon named Benjamin Franklin Stephenson, of Springfield, Illinois, took charge. In April of 1866, he formed an organization of Union veterans that was chartered in

Decatur, Illinois, with just twelve members establishing The Grand Army of the Republic (GAR). By 1890 there were over seven thousand posts throughout the country.[1]

The GAR proposed three objectives: fraternity, charity, and loyalty. Fraternity encouraged veterans to join together in local, state and national meetings, and social events. On July 15, 1875, Scituate area veterans who had served in the Civil War received a charter that formed the George W. Perry Post No. 31, comprising 120 members. Some posts borrowed meeting space from their towns or churches; others bought buildings that were then rented out to other organizations. Scituate was fortunate enough to purchase a former Baptist church turned function hall, called Jenkins Hall. On December 16, 1883, it was rededicated as the Grand Army of the Republic Hall.

GAR Post No. 31 was named in honor of fallen Scituate soldier, George Whitmarsh Perry. Perry was born and raised in Scituate. He served for nine months in the 43rd Regiment Mass. Volunteer Infantry, and he re-enlisted for three years in the 58th Regiment Mass. Volunteer Infantry. Perry was taken prisoner on September 30, 1864, in Virginia, and confined to Salisbury Prison. He died of disease on January 13, 1865, at nineteen years of age in Salisbury, North Carolina.

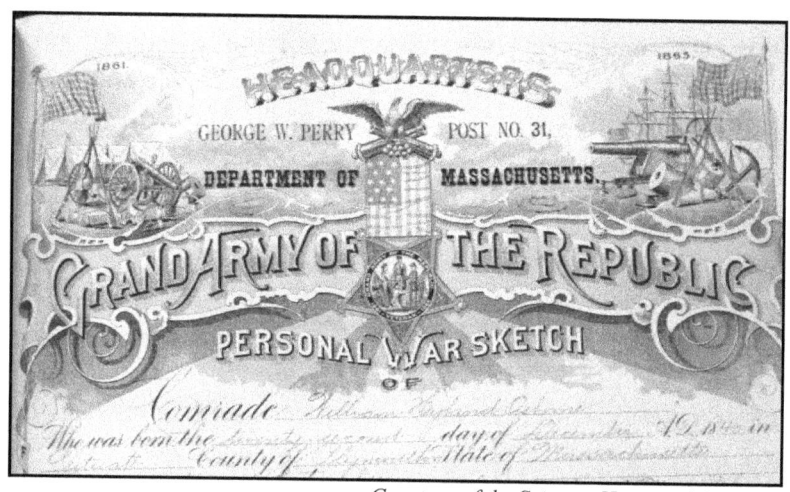

Courtesy of the Scituate Historical Society.

The Scituate Historical Society holds a bound book of the *Personal War Sketches of the Members of the George W. Perry Post No. 31*. George Whitney Merritt was a charter member and the first commander. He served as a private in the 38th Regiment Mass. Volunteer Infantry and as 1st Lieutenant in the 4th Regiment Mass. Heavy Artillery. Merritt represented the district in the Massachusetts Legislature in 1876 and served as a member of the Board of Selectmen for Scituate. He died February 10, 1890, and members Post No. 31 served as escort to his burial.

Civil War Veterans G.A.R. Hall - Picture Taken June 10, 1918.
Courtesy of the Scituate Historical Society.

Back Row - left to right: George Emerson, Edmund F. Merritt, Milton G. Litchfield, Charles H. Nott, Israel D. Damon, Albert Clapp, William T. Clapp and George B. Litchfield.

Front Row - left to right: Charles M. Ferguson, Francis B. Lee, Thomas F. Bailey, James L. Prouty, John H. Towne, Charles Williams and William A. Rathburn.

Benjamin Brown, a charter member, was one of the commanders. He served as a private in the 43rd Regiment Mass. Volunteer Infantry, Company F for nine months, and re-enlisted as a private in the 58th Regiment Mass. Volunteer Infantry. The *Personal War Sketches of the Members of the George W. Perry Post No. 31* states that Brown was, "wounded at Petersburg, Virginia on June 17, 1864, by a musketball through the thigh was taken prisoner and confined at Salisbury, NC," . . . he never recovered but was a great sufferer until his death which occurred January 16, 1893. He was beloved by all his comrades."

William Hyland Osborn(e) also served as a commander of Post No. 31. He was as a private in the 32nd Regiment Mass. Volunteer Infantry, and was wounded at Gettysburg on July 2, 1863. Some of his letters from the Civil War still remain today, and are held in a private collection.

The second objective of the GAR charity, was met in a very practical way, with the GAR setting up funds for the relief of needy veterans, widows, and orphans. This fund was used for medical, burial and housing expenses, and for purchases of food and household goods. Charity was particularly evident in the work of the Woman's Relief Corps that was nationally organized in 1883. On April 5, 1889, the George W. Perry Woman's Relief Corps No. 121, an Auxiliary to Post 31. GAR was founded, and Mrs. Mandana Morris served as the first President. The charter members included Mary F. Prouty, Marion Bailey, Katherine Brown, Agnes Litchfield, and Ida M. Bailey among others.

In the records of the Woman's Relief Corps, held in the Scituate Town Archives, there are accounts of charitable works to benefit veterans and their families. In 1894, the Corps spent $5.00 in relief of Mrs. Pettingale and allotted $1.50 to do "washing" for her as well. Calla lilies were purchased for George Whitaker's funeral, flowers for H. H. Severns' funeral, and later on, "sprays" of flowers for Fred Hyland. In 1895, relief was granted to a soldier's daughter, and in 1897, $2.50 provided clothing for Mrs. Bradley. Fruit and flowers were often provided to veterans, sometimes when they were ill.

Beyond contributions to local families, the Woman's Relief Corps supported regional and national efforts. The Corps supported veterans' hospitals, homes, and health services, as well as orphan's homes. Throughout the years, their donations included money to the Hospital Ship in 1898; sheets, pillows cases, and towels for Soldiers' Dormitory in 1900; in 1921 to John A. Andrew's Home; and in 1922 a large monetary contribution to the Scituate Health Nursing Service. The year 1886 showed donations to the Department Treasurer of the Memorial Home Fund, the National Council of Women, and the Department Treasurer of the Andersonville Stockade Fund, a fund to finance a memorial park at the infamous Andersonville Prison. Also, an annual donation was made to southern areas of the country. In 1899 and again in 1900 funds were donated for the care of the southern graves.

Where did the funds come from? Their records show dues from members but also money raised in 1902 and for many years beyond in penny collections. Other fundraisers were pedlar's parades, harvest fairs, and harvest supplies, and quilt and apron sales. In their two-sided ledger, with receipts on the left and expenses on the right, is a record of the amounts raised. Beginning in 1902, they began, tiny bit by tiny bit, to donate to the Scituate monument fund.

The third objective of the GAR was loyalty, one that was tailor-made for those who had returned home, when others had not. Their goal was to ensure that those who fought were not forgotten and that the lessons learned were not repeated. In 1893 - 1922 the Woman's Relief Corps purchased flags for Union graves, hired a barge for Memorial Day, contributed to the Southern Memorial Fund, and provided flowers for deceased members. In 1922, the flower expense also included flowers for the new monument in Scituate.

Even though the GAR was known for fraternal activities, their pledge of loyalty led to political causes, as posts began to be active in national politics, particularly concerning pensions. Pensions for those permanently disabled were signed into law by President Lincoln in 1862, but by 1879, a more expansive act was signed. It often took the assistance of local posts to help soldiers, widows, and orphans to get help.

In 1914, a local member J. F. Hunt wrote that the Scituate Women's Relief Corps members tried "to be true to the three great principles that govern our order: Faith, Charity and Loyalty. We are ever mindful of our Heroic Dead, and remember them with flowers on each recurring Memorial Day, and thus perpetuate the sacred truth given to us as a duty and privilege, purchased, not by money, but by the blood of those faithful lives who sent out to fight for their Country."

---

[1]. The Library of Congress, Grand Army of the Republic, last modified September 13, 2011, accessed November 15, 2015, http://www.loc.gov/rr/main/gar/garintro.html.

Part III

The Soldiers and Sailors Monument
By Elizabeth Foster

In 1875, the Civil War Veterans from Scituate formed the George W. Perry, Post 31 G.A.R. to recognize the heroism and sacrifices of the men who had fought to preserve the Union. They planned to erect a fitting memorial in the town to honor those who had served so nobly during this war.

While many towns and cities claimed to have celebrated the first "Decoration Day," as Memorial Day was then called, the honor seems to go to Charleston, South Carolina, (ironically, the place where the Civil War had started, with the firing on Fort Sumter by General Beauregard). Near the end of the War, the famous Washington Race Course and Jockey Club, near Charleston, was used as an outdoor prison. "Union soldiers were kept there in horrible conditions in the interior of the track; at least 257 died of exposure and disease and were hastily buried in a mass grave behind the grandstand." After the War ended, "some twenty-eight black workmen, probably recently freed slaves, went to the site, reburied the Union dead properly and built a high fence around the cemetery. They whitewashed the perimeter and built an archway over the entrance, on which they inscribed the words, "Martyrs of the Race Course." On May 1, 1865, a parade of 10,000, led by 3,000 black school children, followed by men, women, and military units including the 54th Massachusetts Colored Regiment, marched to honor the war dead. At the conclusion the attendees picnicked, listened to speeches, and watched military drills. Thus began the custom of honoring our war dead.[1]

On May 1, 1886, General John A. Logan, Commander-in-Chief of the Grand Army of the Republic, called for communities to honor their war dead by decorating their graves with flowers. May 30th was picked as the official date, due to the abundance of flowers at that time of year. Towns and cities around the country picked up the custom of what would later become Memorial Day.[2]

As another way to honor those who fought, memorials sprang up around the country. In Scituate, the issue of the proper site for a monument continued for many years; eventually the Old Meetinghouse Lot, or the Church Common, as it was known, emerged as the choice. The ownership of the land was, however, in question. Did it belong Mr. Thomas Lawson, the G.A.R., or the Town?[3] A most contentious battle ensued between the Town and Mr. Lawson. By 1916, the issue was finally resolved, and a committee was chosen to select a suitable monument. The committee consisted of three veterans: Thomas F. Bailey, James L. Prouty, and John Towne, and two artists: James Hall and William North. Henry Turner Bailey was moderator, but could not vote. From twenty-four entries submitted, the Grand Army veterans chose the design by James Craig of Quincy, while the artists chose a design by A.D. Pickering, claiming it was more "artistic." Henry

---

[1] "The First Decoration Day" Newark Star Ledger, February 11, 2015.
[2] I.b.i.d.
[3] See Willard de Lue, "Tom Lawson Writes the Town Papas"

Turner Bailey resigned saying, "The monument they selected is all right if they would set it up as I suggest. My suggestion is that they dig a hole 30 feet deep and put it in upside down."[4] Even though the majority had voted for the Craig design, and was about to award the contract, when ten citizens stepped forward and applied to the Massachusetts Superior Court for an injunction to stop the process. November 6, 1916, was set as the court date. The artists were supported by the "commuters," and the veterans had the support of the "townies." Fortunately, the veterans had the support of Thomas Lawson, whose father had fought in the Civil War and had died as a result of wounds received. Mr. Lawson wrote letters to the newspapers, had pamphlets printed, but, most importantly, he dispatched his attorney, Homer Alberts, the head of Boston University's Law School, to the hearing. As a result, the veterans won!

Monies were raised by public subscription, donations, and a $10,000 appropriation by the Town of Scituate, and work began.

As we see it today, Mr. Craig's monument stands thirty-three feet high on top of a 14' x 6' base. The shaft is topped with a bronze eagle.
    On the east-facing side above the base are carved the words:

                  Erected in 1917
                    Fraternity
                    Charity
                    Loyalty

Crossed rifles on the right.   Crossed swords on the left.

    On the south-facing aspect is carved:
                Medal of Honor
      Pvt. Charles N. Gardner Company E

---

[4] "My Scituate", Margaret Cole Bonney

32 Massachusetts Infantry[5]
The Medal of Honor is carved as well.
Over this inscription stands the bronze statue of a Civil War soldier.

On the west aspect are the Town Seal and the following inscription:

Erected by the
Town of Scituate
in Memory of its
Soldiers and Sailors
1861-1865

On the right an anchor.   On the left the G.A.R Ribbon.

On the north aspect is carved:
Medal of Honor
Pvt. William H. Osborn
Co. C
29 Massachusetts Infantry[6]

---

[5] Charles Nelson Gardner was born in Scituate, and at the age of 18 this young shoemaker enlisted on 4 August 1862 in the 18th Massachusetts Infantry, Company G as a private. He joined his regiment at Harrison's Landing just prior to the Second Battle of Bull Run. He re-enlisted in 32nd Massachusetts Infantry Co. E. He received his medal for meritorious conduct on capturing an enemy flag at Five Forks, Va. and mustered out on 29 June 1865 and died 22 February 1919. He is buried in Norwell.

[6] William Henry Osborne was born in Scituate and enlisted at the age of 22 in the 29 Regt. Mass Vol. Infantry Company C. He was wounded on 29 June 1865 at Savage's Station, Va; wounded again and taken prisoner, 1 July 1862 at Malvern Hill Va.; discharged for disability on 4 December 1862. The Medal of Honor was awarded for action 1 July 1862 at Malvern Hill, Va. "Although wounded and carried to the rear, he secured a rifle and voluntarily returned to the front, where, failing to find

Courtesy of The Scituate Historical Society.
Pamphlet Cover of Monument Dedication.

The Olmsted Landscape Firm had been hired to landscape the surrounding green space. Trees and plants were all in place on June 17, 1918, when the monument was dedicated with a great

---

his own regiment, he joined another and fought with it until severely wounded and taken prisoner."

deal of fanfare and the help of Thomas Lawson. He was a featured speaker, saying in part:

> For over two decades you veterans of Scituate have struggled for a monument to mark your devotion to your country. Always, as you struggled you have been haunted with the fear that you might all be gone before your monument was born. For the first twenty years after the Civil War it was not heart-clawing to be without a monument. The graves of the dead were kept green by their living comrades...But as another score and a half of years went by the members of your grand old post passed one by one to the Great Beyond...fearful of a day when the last veteran would report to his waiting comrades, "No monument to your memory." Members have come to me with tears in their eyes and the question "What shall we do, what can we do to get our monument before we are all dead." Now the weight is lifted from your hearts...and you can say. We have builded an inspiration-shrine to which can come the ones you loved and the ones who loved you.[7]

Other speakers that day included the Rev. William Ware Locke, Charles W. Peare of the Board of Selectmen, Walter Haynes the Representative from the Second Plymouth District. Miss Marion Bailey read the poem "The Veterans" by Denis A McCarthy. George W. Wilder, Senior Vice-Commander, Dept. of Massachusetts G.A.R., and many others spoke also. The ceremony concluded with Remarks by War Governor Samuel Walker McCall (Lawson's son-in law), a benediction by Rev. Ezra Cox, and, finally the unveiling by Mr. Lawson's daughter, Jennie.

---

[7] Official Program "Dedication of the Soldiers and Sailors Monument, Thomas Lawson speaker.

Courtesy of the Scituate Historical Society.

Even more important than the dignitaries were the fifteen Civil War Veterans in attendance:

All was forgiven, the feud between the "townies" and the "commuters" forgotten, and everyone was happy. In 1921 the Town Meeting voted to name the park after Mr. Lawson.

Thomas Lawson continued to support veterans and to improve the Common, donating fifteen beautiful thirty-year old elms from his estate and purchasing another forty-two mature trees that were planted in 1919 in anticipation of the "Welcome Home Party" for those returning from yet another conflict, the Great War. At 9 a.m. on July 4, 1919, the ceremonies began with the unveiling of a bronze tablet listing those from Scituate who fought in WWI. Mr. Lawson presented the Park to the Town followed by a band concert. After the dedication, Mr. Lawson opened the gates to his beautiful estate and welcomed the whole town to his mansion and grounds for a celebration, consisting of speeches, food, pageants, dinner at the town hall for five hundred guests, dancing at the Dreamwold Coach House (until 1:30 a.m.) and outdoor moving pictures for those not wishing to dance.

Today, the Common continues that spirit of honoring our veterans with the Memorial Day Parade and various other ceremonies, including one at Christmas time; following a brief ceremony at the Soldiers and Sailors Monument, those in attendance walk to Cudworth Cemetery and place Evergreen wreaths on all veterans' graves.

The Common is a beautiful place. Young children splash in the pool; teenagers and young adults throw Frisbees; senior citizens sit on the benches, and all ages walk their dogs. Recently young couples have chosen to have their wedding pictures taken there. It is also a beautiful place just to sit and reflect.

The next time you visit, please take the time to look closely at the monument and thank all those who have fought so bravely for our country.

Part IV

Waldo Turner Letters

Waldo Turner was born in Scituate, on August 22, 1842, to William and Sarah Tilden. He enlisted on August 8, 1862, and mustered on August 19, 1862, as a private in the Massachusetts 35th Infantry Company H for the town of Weymouth, Mass. He was promoted to Full 1st Sergeant on June 9, 1865. He was wounded on December 13, 1862, at Fredericksburg Va., and again on July 30, 1864, at Petersburg Va. He reportedly fought in 17 major battles of the Civil War. He mustered out on June 9, 1865, as a Full 1st Sergeant. Waldo returned to Massachusetts and married a Mary Turner in 1867. He married again in 1902, to Lizzie T. Weston Graves. He served as Commander of the Massachusetts GAR. He died in Weymouth on March 4, 1935.

Waldo Turner Original Letter 1

Camp somewhere about 20 miles outside of Washington in Virginia nobody knows the name of the place and few of us care so long as we can get a days rest. Aug 25th /62

Dear Sister

I take this opportunity to let you know that I am alive and kicking but most (awful) tired it would make quite a little book if I should write you all that has happened to me since I left you just one week ago this morning but I will defer the history of the past week till a more convenient season, we reached Washington yesterday afternoon about 3 o'clk where we had some very black stuff in the shape of a small piece of meat with a piece of ~~two~~ bread the bread was the best I have seen since I have been in the army but the meat.——— dont mention it; if any one had a very quick perception they never would know what it was, but that was not the worst of it after partaking of the bounty given to poor me, we had to sling our knapsacks and budge none of us knew where, over the Potomac we went and kept on marching till nine o'ck when we turned in to a pasture and camped not in tents or houses but on the ground. but nothing but the blue ~~sky~~ sky overhead and Virginy dirt beneath, and by the light of the rising sun we presented an amusing sight,— think if you can of 10 or 12 hundred men after marching 15 or 18 miles in a hot sun with the dust ancle deep in some places and even then you can form no idea of how we looked,

But I have had no harder time than I expected to when I enlisted, I am now writing in an old meeting house called Winters chapel formally the property of the rebels.... the man is waiting for the letters and I must close when we get settled I'll write and tell you the whole story, yours &c
Waldo

Direct Waldo Sun Co H, 35 Reg Mass Vol Washington D C care of Col

Waldo Turner Letter 1 Transcribed

August 25, '62

Dear Sister,

 I take this opportunity to let you know that I am alive and kicking but most (awful) tired. It would make quite a little book if I should write you all that has happened to me since I left you just one week ago this morning but - I will defer the history of the past week till a more convenient season, we reached Washington yesterday afternoon about 3 o'clock when we had some very black stuff in the shape of a small piece of meat - with a piece of bread. The bread was the best I have seen since I have been in the army but the meat - don't mention it, if anyone had a very quick perception (illegible) they never would know what it was, but that was not the worst of it - after fortaking of the bounty given to poor me we had to sling our knapsacks and budge (?). None of us knew where, over the Potomac we went and kept on marching till nine o'clock when we turned into a pasture and camped not in tents or houses but on the ground, but nothing but the blue sky overhead and Virginia dirt beneath and by the light of the rising sun we presented an amusing sight. Think if you can of 10 or 12 hundred men after marching 15 or 18 miles in a hot sun with the dust and (illegible) in some places and even then you can form an idea of how we looked.

 But I have had no harder time than I expected to when I enlisted. I am now writing in an old meeting house called Hunters chapel formally the property of the rebels. The man is waiting for the letters and I must close. When we get settled I'll write and tell you the whole story.

Yours vt,
Waldo

Direct Waldo Turner Co. #35 Regiment Mass (illegible)
Washington DC Care of Capt. Pratt

Letter 2 from Waldo Turner to his sister Eudora

Bealeton Station, VA
May 3, 1864

My dear Sister:

I take this opportunity to write you once more as it is rumored that we are off again in the morning so I shall not have time to write then...we came here the 31st three days from Alexandria. I wrote you late one night at Fairfax CH (?) to let you know that I was well. I will now write you a few particulars of our march. We left Annapolis April 23 and marched to Washington and was reviewed by Gen'l Burnside and President Lincoln from a balcony of Willards Hotel on the corner of Pennsylvania Ave and Fourteenth Sts. The Gen'l looked as merry and cheerful as ever and his ruddy healthy face was in strange contrast with the hollow sunken look of cheeks and careworn look of the President. This is the first time that I have ever had the chance to see him not withstanding I spent nearly 8 months in W. last year. One can but pity him to see how the duties of his office wear upon him and I thought while passing in review that although my knapsack seemed as though it would break my back I was so tired, that I had rather tote that then have the load of care that he has to bear night and day. We crossed Long Bridge the same day and marched to near Alexandria and camped one day and two nights and then started on another march and arrived at Fairfax the same day and then I wrote you. the next day we marched through Centerville and across the plains of Mannasses (sp?) finding Bull Run and crossing the battle field about noon the old earthworks are still visible and trees are all scarred with bullet wounds but that is all. The grass is shining fresh and green and little remains to be seen of the awful strife of 61 & 2. The country from Centerville to Mannassas green (?) must have been one of the finest in the state before the war. It is the name indicates a vast plain but is now a howling wilderness..whose only inhabitants are small bands of guerrillas who get there living by murder and robbery. Woe to the unlucky wagon train that dares venture through here unguarded or to the poor soldier who struggles. they take all the horses and everything of value and either butcher the men or strip them of everything and send them onto us with the comforting assurance that they will be shot the next time they are caught. We arrived at Bristoe Station that night and bivouacked. The nexty day we crossed Broad River and came by Catlett (?) Station and Warrenton Junction relieving the troops of the fifth corps and sending them to the front leaving some of our Corps in their places and camped for the night in nearly the same place that we did sixteen months ago on the the march from Sulphur Springs to Fredericksburg. The next day we came here and relieved the troops here and laid out our camp and entered upon some new business (to us) ie guarding the Orange & Alexandria Railroad. Great preparation are being made for the coming campaign they average about one train an hour here all day and night with supplies for the army. I hear that Meade has crossed the Rapidan and that the whole army is on the move. We have orders to be ready to move at an hours notice as we are a kind of reserve we cannot tell where we shall go whereever they want us they will send us I suppose. At any rate it don't worry me at all. I am ready. I have seen the folly of borrowing trouble and learned to take things as they come. We have been made a part of the 1st Brigades's 1st Div. and in fact the whole Div. is made up of Massachusetts troops and is commanded by a Major General (Stephenson) the 36 & 7 & 9th Mass are in the same Brigade with us and our General commands the Brigade. Did you say Frank Nickols was in the 39th? What Co.? I shall hunt him up as soon as possible ... is there any other Scituate boys that I know there? There are two Weymouth boys in the 38th that I used to know. We expect the 38th here every day. My health is verry (sp) good at present. Don't fret yourself to any unnecessary uneasiness on my account. Remember that he who careth for the lilies of the field will not forget to care for me and will deal with me as seemeth him good. Remember me *kindly to all. Give my love to Ara and her family and believe me as ever your loving Brother.*

Waldo

P.S. I believe I have sent you a picture please give this one to Ara. Waldo

<u>Transcriber's comment</u>: "Ara" was probably Arabella, older sister of Eudora and Waldo.

Wallet, photo and letters courtesy of private collection.

Waldo carried this wallet with him throughout the war.

Part V

Compiled list of Scituate Soldiers and Sailors

August Ahlborn
A millwright from Buffalo, New York, he was 29 years old when he enlisted and mustered into service for 3 years in the 7th Battery Mass. Volunteer Artillery on January 30, 1864. August received a $125 bounty from the town.

James Theodore Johnson Andrews
James was born in Boston, April 14, 1845, to parents Christopher and Hannah (Damon) Andrews. He worked as a clerk. James enlisted July 7, 1862, as a private in the 35th Regiment Mass. Volunteer Infantry, Company A for three years and mustered in August 9, 1862. He received a $100 bounty from the town. He died on February 4, 1863, in a camp near Falmouth, Virginia of convulsions, after being sick for sixteen hours.

Ruben Snow Hayden Andrews
Ruben was born in Boston, January 15, 1839, to parents Christopher and Hannah (Damon) Andrews. He worked as a laborer. Ruben enlisted August 4, 1862, as a private in the 35th Regiment Mass. Volunteer Infantry, Company A for 3 years and mustered in August 9, 1862. He received a $100 bounty from the town. On June 9, 1865, he mustered out of service at Alexandria, Virginia.

William Baker Damon Andrews

William was born in Boston, April 10, 1843, to parents Christopher and Hannah (Damon) Andrews. He worked as a clerk. William enlisted June 16, 1862, as a private in the 35th Regiment Mass. Volunteer Infantry, Company A for three years and mustered in August 9, 1862. He received $100 bounty from the town. He was promoted to corporal May 20, 1863, and full sergeant June 20, 1864. On September 30, 1864, William was killed at the Battle of Cedar Creek, Virginia.

Alfred Arago

28 year-old, gunsmith from Springfield, Massachusetts, Alfred mustered into service on December 7, 1864, in 1st Regiment Mass. Volunteer Cavalry, Company H. He received a $125 bounty from the town.

James Ba(e)rry

James was born in Ireland to parents John and Joanna. He was resident of Scituate and worked as a laborer and farmer when he enlisted on August 4, 1862, for three years and mustered into service on August 20, 1862, as a private in the 38th Regiment Mass. Volunteer Infantry, Company G. He received a $100 bounty from the town. James mustered out of service on June 30, 1865.

James Anson Bailey

James Anson was born in Dorchester, Massachusetts on September 15, 1832, to parents Sewall and Eliza. He was married and a resident of Scituate, working as a shoemaker when he enlisted on January 1, 1864, for three years and mustered into service on January 24, 1864, as a private in the 9th Regiment Mass. Volunteer Battery. He mustered out of service on June 6, 1865.

John William Bailey

John was born in East Boston on October 23, 1842, to parents Edwin and Margret (Dyas) Bailey; John William was a resident of Scituate. He worked as a farmer. On August 11, 1862, he enlisted for three years and mustered into service on September 2, 1862, in 39th Regiment Mass. Volunteer Infantry, Company G as a private. On June 2, 1865, he mustered out of service. He was a charter member of Post 31, G.A.R. His G.A.R. profile states that he died at Scituate May 27, 1884, and was buried in Chelsea. At the funeral services his body was enwrapped in

"Old Glory" according to his request. An escort of eight comrades of the Post accompanied the remains to the burial. He participated in the battles of Brock Pike, Laurel Hill, North Anna River, White Oak Swamp, Weldon Railroad and Petersburg.

Joseph Jr. Bailey

Joseph Jr. was born in Scituate on September 10, 1822, to parents Joseph and Sarah White (Wood) Bailey. He was married and worked as a carpenter. He enlisted on January 1, 1864, for three years and mustered into service on January 24, 1864, as a private in the 9th Battery Mass. Volunteer Light Artillery. He mustered out of service on June 6, 1865.

Jotham Wade Bailey

Jotham Wade was born in Scituate on May 5, 1832, to parents Thomas Tilden and Hannah (Wade) Bailey. He was married and worked in shoe manufacturing. He enlisted on September 2, 1862, for 9 months and mustered into service on September 12, 1862, as a corporal in the 43rd Regiment Mass. Volunteer Infantry, Company F. He received a $100 bounty from the town. On Nov. 8, 1862, he was discharged due to disability. Jotham paid back the $100 bounty to the town.

Samuel Mills Bailey

Samuel was born in East Boston on October 17, 1844, to parents Edwin and Margret. A resident of Scituate, he worked as a carpenter and mustered into service in October 1861 as a private for 3 years. He served in the 10th Regiment, Company D of the Illinois Cavalry. He died on October 15, 1863, at Little Rock, Arkansas of dysentery.

Seth Kent Bailey

Seth Kent was born in Scituate on March 28, 1817, to parents Amasa and Sally F. (Kent) Bailey., and worked as carpenter. He enlisted on August 4, 1862, for three years and mustered into service on August 20, 1862, as a private in the 38th Regiment Mass. Volunteer Infantry, Company G. He received a $100 bounty from the town. On September 6, 1862, Seth Kent died in camp at Baltimore, Maryland of dysentery.

Thomas Tilden Bailey

Thomas Tilden was born in Scituate on February 21, 1830, to Thomas Tilden and Hannah (Wade) Bailey. He was married and worked as a trader. He enlisted and mustered into service on August 11, 1862, as a private in the 7th Regiment Mass. Volunteer Infantry, Company K. He received a $100 bounty from the town.

John Barrows

John Barrows, a cook, enlisted on January 14, 1862, at Boston for 3 years in the U.S. Navy. He was credited to the quota of the town of Scituate. He served as seaman on the *Ohio* and *USS Kearsarge*, from which he was discharged November 30, 1864.

George W. Bass

George W. Bass, a 39-year-old machinist, enlisted August 20, 1864, and served in the 1st Louisiana Calvary mustering out of service on September 11, 1865. He was listed as part of the contraband soldiers added to the Scituate quota. He received a $125 bounty from the town.

Charles Elliott Bates

Charles Elliott was born on November 10, 1839, in Scituate to parents Peter E. and Sophia (Jenkins) Bates. He worked as a laborer and fisherman. He enlisted on August 6, 1861, in the 1st Regiment Mass. Volunteer Heavy Artillery, Company A. On December 4, 1861, he was discharged for disability at Fort Albany, Virginia. He re-enlisted on August 4, 1862, for 3 years and mustered into service on Aug. 20, 1862, as a private in the 38th Regiment Mass. Volunteer Infantry, Company G. He received a $100 bounty from the town. On February 3, 1863, he was discharged for disability at Baltimore, Maryland.

Charles Eugene Bates

Charles Eugene was born in Cohasset on December 16, 1837, to parents Charles and Clara (Turner) Bailey. He was a resident of Scituate and worked as a farmer and boatman. He enlisted on August 11, 1862, for 3 years and mustered into service on September 2, 1862, as a private in the 39th Regiment Mass. Volunteer Infantry, Company G. He was wounded in the left arm on May 8, 1864, at the Battle of Laurel Hill, Virginia. Charles Eugene died of disease on November 2, 1864, in Baltimore, Maryland.

George Hurbert Bates

George Hurbert was born on May 3, 1839, in Topsfield, Massachusetts to parents George W. and Celia; he worked as a schoolteacher and printer. He enlisted on August 4, 1862, for 3 years and mustered into service on August 20, 1862, in 38th Regiment Mass. Volunteer Infantry, Company G. He received a bounty of $100 from the town. On November 1, 1862, he was promoted to 1st sergeant. George Hurbert was discharged for disability due to dysentery on April 3, 1863, Algiers, Louisiana as 1st sergeant. He re-enlisted on July 9, 1864, for 100 days and mustered into service on July 20, 1864, in the 42nd Regiment Mass. Volunteer Infantry, Company D. He was commissioned as a 1st lieutenant in July 1864. On November 11, 1864, he mustered out of service.

George Sherman Bates

George Sherman, a mason, born November 10, 1841, in Scituate to Peter E. and Sophia (Jenkins) Bates, enlisted on December 7, 1863, for one year at Boston. He served as a seaman on the *Ohio*, *USS Ticonderago*, *Conemaugh* and *Richmond* and was discharged December 31, 1864. Bates had previously served for nine months in the 43rd Mass. Regiment Volunteer Infantry, Company F.

Orrin Bates

Orrin, a shoemaker, was born in Marshfield on April 3, 1845, to parents Marshall and Huldah (Hall) Bates. On July 9, 1864, he enlisted for 100 days and mustered into service on July 20, 1864, in the 42nd Regiment Mass. Volunteer Infantry, Company D. On November 11, 1864, he mustered out of service.

William Bates

William, a caulker and graver, was born on August 16, 1828, in Scituate to parents John and Sally (Northey) Bates. On July 9, 1864, he enlisted for 100 days and mustered into service on July 20, 1864, in the 42nd Regiment Mass. Volunteer Infantry, Company D. On November 11, 1864, he mustered out of service.

Roswell R.D. Bell

A 33-year-old farmer in Scituate, Roswell enlisted on April 2, 1864, for three years. He was mustered into service on April 12, 1864, as a private in the 5th Regiment Mass. Volunteer Cavalry. He received $125 from the town and $25 from private funds. He was discharged from a hospital in Fort Monroe, Virginia on June 12, 1865.

Matthew Blair

A 27-year-old farmer from Tyson, VT, Matthew enlisted on January 22, 1864, for three years. He mustered into service on February 4, 1864, in the 56th Regiment Mass. Volunteer Infantry, Company I. He received $125 from the town. Matthew died June 18, 1864 of wounds received June 17, 1864, at Petersburg, Virginia. He also served in Company B of the 13th Vermont Infantry.

William James Bouve

William was born in Scituate on July 14, 1845, to parents Sylvanus and Mary (Jenkins) Bouve. He worked as a laborer. On September 12, 1862, he mustered into service as a private for 9 months in the 43rd Regiment Mass. Volunteer Infantry, Company F. He received $100 bounty from the town. On July 30, 1863, he was discharged.

George Nelson Bramhall

George a mariner, resident of Scituate, and born in Boston in 1840 enlisted October 7, 1861, at New Bedford for three years in the U.S. Navy. He served as a seaman on the *Ohio*, *USS Augusta*, and *Commodore Read* and was discharged October 6, 1864. Bramhall enlisted again on October 7, 1864, at Washington D.C. and served for one year on the *Ohio* and *USS Commodore Read*. He was discharged June 3, 1865.

Bela Francis Brown

Bela was born in Scituate on April 23, 1841, to parents John and Clarissa (Cook) Brown. He worked as a jeweler and watchmaker and mustered into service on August 18, 1862, as a private for 3 years in the 22nd Regiment Mass. Volunteer Infantry, Company C. On December 13, 1862, in Fredericksburg, Virginia and on May 10, 1864, in the Battle of Chancellorsville, Laurel Hill, Virginia. Bela was wounded in the arm, neck, and leg (which was later amputated). He died May 17, 1864, at Washington, D.C. of the wound in the neck.

Benjamin Brown

A resident of Scituate, Benjamin was born in Boston on August 10, 1828, to parents Benjamin and Margret (Holbrook) Brown. He was married and worked as a caulker and graver. He enlisted on September 2, 1862, and mustered into service on September 12, 1862, in the 43rd Regiment Mass. Volunteer Infantry, Company F for nine months. He mustered out of service on July 30, 1863. On March 17, 1864, he re-enlisted and mustered into service on May 13, 1864, in the 58th Regiment Mass. Volunteer Infantry, Company I for three years. He received $125 bounty from the town. On June 17, 1864, he was wounded at Petersburg, Virginia by a musket ball in the thigh and taken prisoner on September 30, 1864, at Popular Grove, Virginia and confined to Salisbury Prison. He was exchanged on March 9, 1865, and mustered out on July 14, 1865.

Charles Edward Brown

Charles was a resident of Scituate born on June 30, 1828, to parents Charles and Martha (Lufkin) Brown in Cape Ann, Massachusetts. He was married and worked as a mason. He enlisted on September 2, 1862, for 9 months and mustered in September 12, 1862, as a 43rd Regiment Mass. Volunteer Infantry Company F. He received a $100 bounty paid by the town. James mustered out July 30, 1863.

Elisha James Brown

Elisha was born in Scituate on June 7, 1839, to parents Abel and Judith (Lufkin) Brown. He worked as a shoemaker and mustered into service February 22, 1862, as a private for 3 years in the 32nd Regiment Mass. Volunteer Infantry, Company F. He was a charter member of Post 31, G.A.R. He participated in the battles of Antietam and Fredericksburg (per G.A.R. profiles). He was discharged for disability March 13, 1863, at Boston, Massachusetts.

Everett Edward Brown

Everett was born October 29, 1845, in Scituate to parents Samuel and Harriet F. (Clapp) Brown. He was married and worked as a shoemaker. Everett enlisted July 9, 1864, for 100 days and mustered July 20, 1864, into the 42nd Regiment Mass. Volunteer Infantry, Company D. He mustered out November 11, 1864. Five months later, Everett enlisted and mustered for 1 year on April 7, 1865, in the 62nd Regiment Mass.

Volunteer Infantry, Company A. He received a bounty of $125 from the town. He mustered out May 5, 1865.

George Davis Brown

George was born in Scituate on November 28, 1838, to parents John and Clarissa (Cook) Brown. He worked as a nailcutter and mustered into service on May 22, 1861, as a private for 3 years in the 29th Regiment Mass. Volunteer Infantry, Company C. He was killed June 15, 1862, while on picket duty at Fair Oaks, Virginia.

Henry Brown

Henry a 42-year-old from Norwich, Massachusetts mustered in February 22, 1864. He served in the 5th Regiment Mass. Volunteer Cavalry. He received $125 bounty from the town.

Henry Brown

Henry was born on March 5, 1834, in Scituate to parents Samuel and Louisa (Clapp) Brown. He was married and worked as a shoemaker and caulker. He mustered into service on August 20, 1862 for three years as a private in the 38th Regiment Mass. Volunteer Infantry, Company D. Henry mustered out of service July 13, 1864, to enlist in the U.S. Navy, and served on the *Portsmouth*, and was discharged from Chelsea Hospital on April 22, 1865.

Henry Lewis Brown

Henry Lewis was born in Scituate June 6, 1842, to parents Lewis and Lydia B. (Hyland) Brown. He worked as a cordwainer and shoemaker. He enlisted on September 2, 1862, for 9 months and mustered in September 12, 1862, as a private in the 43rd Regiment Mass. Volunteer Infantry, Company F. He received a $100 bounty paid by town and mustered out July 30, 1863.

James Brown

James enlisted January 30, 1864. He served in the 3rd Regiment Mass. Volunteer Cavalry. He received $125 bounty from the town.

James Lufkin Brown

James was a resident of Scituate born on October 29, 1830, in Cape Ann, MA to parents Charles and Martha (Lufkin) Brown. He was married and worked as a shoemaker. On August 12, 1862, he enlisted, and he mustered in August 20, 1862, as a private for 3 years in the 38th Regiment Mass. Volunteer Infantry, Company G receiving a $100 bounty paid by the town. James was discharged for disability July 23, 1863, in New Orleans, Louisiana (dysentery for three months) and died August 4, 1863, in the St. James General Hospital New Orleans.

Joseph Brown

Joseph was born in Scituate on October 26, 1814, to parents Joseph and Mercy (Litchfield) Brown. He was married and worked as a shoemaker and bootmaker. On February 24, 1862, Joseph mustered in as a Private for three years in the 32nd Regiment Mass. Volunteer Infantry, Company F. He was transferred to Veteran Reserve Corps (V.R.C.), September 1, 1863, and mustered out of Co. "A" 18th V.R.C. on Feb. 24, 1865.

Joseph Howard Brown

Joseph was born on June 28, 1842, in Scituate to parents Joseph Jr. and Emily (Clapp) Brown. He worked as a shoemaker. On August 9, 1864, he mustered in as a private for one year in the 4th Regiment Mass. Heavy Artillery, Company C. He received a bounty of $125 from the town and $75 from a private source. He was mustered out June 17, 1865.

Thomas Carreggio Brown

A resident of Scituate, Thomas was born in New York City on June 3, 1840, to parents Daniel and Elizabeth (Ball) Brown. He worked as a shoe stitcher. On April 18, 1864, he mustered into service as a private for three years in the 58th Regiment Mass. Volunteer Infantry, Company E. He received $125 bounty from the town and was discharged July 14, 1863.

Wilbur Parker Brown

Wilbur was born January 8, 1848, in Gloucester, Massachusetts to parents Charles II and Martha. He worked as a farmer. He enlisted for 100 days on July 9, 1864 and mustered in July 20, 1864, as a private in the 42nd Regiment Mass. Volunteer Infantry, Company D. He was discharged on November 11, 1864.

Michael Buckley

A 32-year-old resident of Gloucester, Massachusetts, Michael worked as a laborer. He enlisted and mustered into service for three years on March 26, 1864, as a private in the 35th Regiment Mass. Volunteer Infantry, Company I. He received $125 bounty from the town and $25 from private funds. He was wounded on May 5, 1864, in The Battle of the Wilderness, Virginia and transferred to the Veteran Reserve Corps (V.R.C.) on Nov. 27, 1864. Michael mustered out on July 25, 1865, from Company G of the 14th V.RC.; he had prior service in Company B of the 10th Maine Infantry.

Thomas M. Burnett

Thomas, a fisherman, born April 1, 1845, in Scituate to parents Thomas W. (a sailor) and Mary A., enlisted November 16, 1863, at Boston for one year in the U.S. Navy. Burnett served as a landsman on the *Ohio*, *USS Connecticut*, and the *Hendrick Hudson*. He was discharged November 29, 1864.

William Thomas Burrows (Burroughs)

William Thomas was a stair builder born November 22, 1841, in Scituate to parents Thomas J. and Betsey W. (Vinal) Burrows. He enlisted December 8, 1863, at Boston for one year in the U.S. Navy. He served as a seaman on the *Ohio*, and the *USS Niphon*. He was discharged from North Carolina on December 6, 1864. His father, Thomas J., was a mariner in Scituate. Captain of the *Argus*. He died at sea.

Francis B. Burton

Francis was 24 years old and a resident from Middletown, New York. He listed his occupation as a wheelwright. Francis enlisted and mustered into service on March 24, 1864, as a Private in the 28th Regiment Mass. Volunteer Infantry, Company I. He received a bounty of $125 from the town and $25 from private funds. Francis was discharged from Company E on June 30, 1865.

Henry Harrison Chubbuck

Henry Harrison was born in Scituate on October 1, 1840, to parents Anthony and Cynthia (Merritt) Chubbuck. He worked as a mason. On September 16, 1862, he mustered into the 43rd Mass. Volunteer Infantry, Company K as a private for 9 months. He received a $100 bounty paid by the town and mustered out of service July 30, 1863. He re-enlisted

December 9, 1863 and mustered into service December 22, 1863, for three years in the 2nd Regiment Mass. Volunteer Heavy Artillery. He was promoted to corporal on March 18, 1864, and mustered out September 3, 1865.

Albert Clapp

Albert was born November 22, 1842, in Scituate to parents Rufus and Nancy (Hall) Clapp. He worked as a farmer. On August 10, 1864, he enlisted and mustered into service for one year as a private in the 4th Regiment Mass. Volunteer Heavy Artillery, Company C. He received a $125 bounty from the town and $75 from private funds. Albert was mustered out June 17, 1865.

Charles Henry Clapp

Charles Henry was born in Scituate September 15, 1842, to parents Charles and Anna W. He worked as a stage driver and enlisted November 2, 1861, for three years. He mustered in November 26, 1861, as a private in the 32nd Regiment Mass. Volunteer Infantry, Company A. On February 22, 1863, in Potomac Creek at a camp near Falmouth, Virginia, Charles Henry died of congestion of the lungs after being sick one day.

Charles Whitcomb Clapp

Charles was born November 2, 1835, in Scituate to parents Harvey and Hannah (Whitcomb) Clapp. He worked as a shoemaker. He enlisted and mustered into service on June 15, 1861, for three years as a private in the 7th Regiment Mass. Volunteer Infantry, Company K. He was discharged July 19, 1862, due to rheumatism. On August 9, 1864, he enlisted and mustered into the 4th Regiment Mass. Volunteer Heavy Artillery, Company C. He mustered out June 17, 1865, as a sergeant.

Henry Oscar Clapp

Henry Oscar was born in Scituate on April 15, 1847, to parents Henry (a merchant) and Frances (Perry) Clapp. He worked as a clerk and enlisted on September 2, 1862, as a private for 9 months. He mustered in September 12, 1862, in the 43rd Regiment Mass. Volunteer Infantry, Company F. He received a $100 bounty paid by the town and mustered out July 30, 1863. Henry re-enlisted July 9, 1864, and mustered into service on July 20, 1864, in the 42nd Regiment Mass. Volunteer Infantry, Company D for 100 Days as a sergeant. He mustered out Nov. 11, 1864.

Henry Thomas Clapp

Henry was born in Scituate on April 1, 1840, to parents Thomas and Ann R. (Cudworth) Clapp. He worked as a farmer and, also, listed his occupation as a photographer. He enlisted on July 9, 1864, and mustered into service July 20, 1864, for 100 days in the 42nd Regiment Mass. Volunteer Infantry, Company D. Henry mustered out November 11, 1864.

Peleg Ford Clapp

Peleg Ford was born in Scituate on January 27, 1835, to parents Elijah III and Harriet (Ford) Clapp. He worked as a mason and enlisted September 2, 1862, for 9 months. He mustered in September 12, 1862, in the 43rd Regiment Mass. Volunteer Infantry, Company F as a 2nd sergeant. He received a $100 bounty paid by the town. Discharged May 29, 1863, he re-enlisted in the 2nd Mass. Heavy Artillery and was Commissioned 2nd lieutenant on June 4, 1863. He re-enlisted once again in the 16th Battery Mass. Volunteer Artillery on March 4, 1864, and mustered into service March 11, 1864. He was appointed sergeant on March 31, 1864, and 1st sergeant on April 13, 1865. He mustered out June 27, 1865.

William Thomas Clapp

William was born in Scituate on August 6, 1844, to parents Harvey (shoemaker) and Hannah (Whitcomb) Clapp. He was a farmer in Scituate. He enlisted and mustered into service on August 9, 1864, for 1 year in the 4th Regiment Mass. Volunteer Heavy Artillery, Company C. He received $125 bounty from the town and $75 from private funds. William mustered out June 17, 1865.

Henry Otis Cole

Henry Otis was born in August 2, 1844, to parents Joseph O. and Sarah W. (Prouty) Cole. He listed his occupation as a scholar and enlisted on August 4, 1862, for three years. He mustered in August 20, 1862, as a private in 38th Regiment Mass. Volunteer Infantry, Company G. He received a $100 bounty paid by the town. Henry Otis was promoted to sergeant September 1, 1863, and promoted to 1st sergeant June 1, 1865. Henry mustered out June 30, 1865.

John Nelson Collier

John Nelson, a resident of Scituate, was born January 16, 1832, in Pawtucket, Rhode Island to parents David and Delana. He was a clergyman and was married. He mustered in September 16, 1862, as a corporal for 9 months in the 43rd Mass. Volunteer Infantry, Company K. He received a $100 bounty paid by the town and mustered out of service July 30, 1863.

Harvey Conlyn

Harvey was a 22-year-old resident of Boston when he enlisted. He worked as a laborer. On May 19, 1864, he enlisted and mustered into service in the 2nd Regiment Mass. Volunteer Infantry. He received $125 bounty from the town and an additional $25 from private funds.

Christopher Conrad

Christopher was a 35-year-old resident of Boston when he enlisted. He worked as a sailor. On March 24, 1864, he enlisted and mustered into service in the 19th Regiment Mass. Volunteer Infantry, Company C. He received $125 bounty from the town and $25 from private funds. On May 7, 1864, he was reported missing at Wilderness, Virginia and later died of disease April 2, 1865, at Harewood Hospital, Washington D.C.

Bernard Conway

Bernard was a 28-year-old resident of Providence, Rhode Island when he enlisted. He worked as a laborer. On March 29, 1864, he mustered into the 19th Regiment Mass. Volunteer Infantry, Company C. He received a bounty of $125 from the town and $25 from private funds. He was wounded on May 6, 1864, at Wilderness, Virginia. Bernard returned to duty from the hospital on July 15, 1864.

Francis Marion Cook

Francis Marion Cook, a mariner, born in Scituate September 11, 1838, to Josiah H. F. and Philenda (Little) Cook, enlisted November 26, 1863, at San Francisco for one year and served as a landsman on the *USS Narragansett*.

George Henry Cook

George was born November 18, 1843, in Scituate to parents Russell (a tailor) and Mary V. (Otis) Cook. He worked as a glasscutter. On November 1, 1861, he enlisted and mustered into service for three years as a private in the 3rd Mass. Volunteer Cavalry, Company L. He was part of the Magee's Mounted Rifle Rangers. On June 11, 1862, George was discharged for disability.

Langdon Williams Cook

Langdon was born September 25, 1847, in Scituate to parents Samuel and Sarah L. (Whitcomb) Cook. He worked as a shoemaker and farmer. He mustered into service for 100 days on July 20, 1864, as a private in the 42nd Regiment Mass. Volunteer Infantry, Company D. Langdon mustered out on November 11, 1864.

Samuel William Cook

Samuel was born in Scituate on April 4, 1819, to parents Ichabod and Mary (Sutton) Cook. He was married and worked as a shoemaker. He enlisted on August 4, 1862, and mustered in August 20, 1862, as a private for three years in the 38th Regiment Mass. Volunteer Infantry, Company G. He received a $100 bounty paid by town. He was discharged for disability in Boston on August 6, 1864.

William Ambrose Cook

William was born on February 22, 1835, in Scituate to parents William and Elisa (Merritt) Cook. He worked as a mason. He enlisted and mustered into service on June 15, 1861, for three years as a private in the 7th Regiment Mass. Volunteer Infantry, Company K. William was discharged on April 17, 1863, at a camp near Falmouth, Virginia due to disability.

James Winchell Cudworth

James was born on September 12, 1824, in Scituate to parents Israel and Mabel (Jenkins) Cudworth. He was married and worked as a boat builder. He enlisted on July 9, 1864, for 100 Days and mustered into service on July 20, 1864, as a private in the 42nd Regiment Mass. Volunteer Infantry, Company D. He mustered out November 11, 1864.

Job Edwin Curtis

Job was born October 12, 1842, in Scituate to parents Norton and Mary P. (Chessbrook) Curtis. He worked as shoemaker. He enlisted and mustered on August 10, 1864, as a private for one year into the 4th Regiment Mass. Volunteer Heavy Artillery, Company C. He mustered out June 17, 1865.

Shadrach Briggs Curtis

Shadrach was born September 22, 1823, in Scituate to parents Shadrach and Anna (Cudworth) Curtis. He worked as a mariner. He enlisted and mustered into service on January 4, 1864, for three years as a private in the 9th Battery Mass. Volunteer Light Artillery. He mustered out June 12, 1865, at Washington, D.C.

John Peak Cushing

John was born March 19, 1836, in Scituate to parents Nathaniel and Olive (Wade) Cushing. He worked as a blacksmith. He enlisted April 15, 1861, for three months and mustered into service on April 30, 1861 as a private in the 8th Regiment Mass. Volunteer Militia, Company A. He mustered out August 1, 1861. He re-enlisted on August 24, 1861, and mustered into the 19th Regiment Mass. Volunteer Infantry, Company H on August 28, 1861, as a corporal. He was transferred to Company I in December 1861. John was wounded June 30, 1862, at the Battle of White Oak Swamp, near Glendale, Virginia. The next day he was taken prisoner and carried to Richmond, Virginia. John was paroled on July 27, 1862, in a prisoner exchange, and was discharged for disability in Washington, D.C. on November 29, 1862.

Samuel Price Dalby (Dolby)

Samuel was born October 22, 1842, in Roxbury, MA to parents John and Cynthia. He worked as a shoemaker. He enlisted and mustered into service on August 9, 1864, for one year as a private in 4th Regiment Mass. Volunteer Heavy Artillery, Company C. He was discharged for disability at Fort Richardson, Virginia on February 18, 1865.

Alfred Caleb Damon

Alfred was born March 6, 1836, in Scituate to parents Issac Baker and Mary Ann (Hayden) Damon. He was married and worked as a cordwainer and shoemaker. He mustered into service on September 12, 1862, for 9 months as a private in the 43rd Regiment Mass. Volunteer Infantry, Company F receiving a $100 bounty from the town. Alfred mustered out July 30, 1863.

Andrew Jackson Damon

Andrew was born June 14, 1843, in Scituate to John C. and Polly R. (Mayo) Damon. He worked as a shoemaker and mason. He enlisted on August 11, 1862, and mustered into service on September 2, 1862, in the 39th Regiment Mass. Volunteer Infantry, G. He was discharged at Boston on July 31, 1863, for dysentery and phthisis (another name for tuberculosis).

Edwin White Damon

Edwin was born April 8, 1837, in Scituate to John and Almira (White) Damon. He worked as a mason. He enlisted on November 6, 1861, at Boston and served in the U.S. Engineer Corps, Company C for three years. He left sick at Haxall's Landing, Virginia on July 1, 1862, and was reported missing July 12, 1862, and presumed dead.

Israel Davis Damon

Israel was born May 9, 1844, in Scituate to Israel and Susan (Farrington) Damon. He worked as a farmer. He enlisted on September 2, 1862, for 9 months and mustered into service September 12, 1862, in the 43rd Regiment Mass. Volunteer Infantry, Company F. He received a $100 bounty from the town. Israel was mustered out July 30, 1863.

Virgil Damon

Virgil was born September 27, 1823, to parents Josiah Jr. and Mary (Webb) Damon. He was married and worked as a farmer and blacksmith. He enlisted on September 2, 1862, for 9 months and mustered into service on September 12, 1862, as a private in the 43rd Regiment Mass. Volunteer Infantry, Company F. He received a bounty of $100 from the town. Virgil mustered out July 30, 1863.

William Rogers Damon

William was born in Marshfield, Massachusetts on April 20, 1829, to parents Isaac B. and MaryAnn Elizabeth (Hayden) Damon. He was married and worked as a shoemaker. He enlisted and mustered into service on August 6, 1862, for three years as a private in the 18th Regiment Mass. Volunteer Infantry, Company G. He was wounded

December 13, 1862, in Fredericksburg, VA. He was promoted to corporal March 1, 1863, and sergeant Nov. 25, 1863. On December 23, 1863, William re-enlisted and mustered in January 1, 1864, in the 18th Regiment Mass. Volunteer Infantry, Company G. He was promoted to sergeant November 25, 1863, he transferred October 21, 1864, to the 32rd Regiment Mass. Volunteer Infantry, Company L. He mustered out June 13, 1865.

Riley Danforth

Riley was a 30 year-old farmer from Scituate. He mustered into service on February 4, 1864, as a private in the 59th Regiment Mass. Volunteer Infantry, Company E. He received a bounty of $125 from the town.

John Doherty

John was born in New York City on August 17, 1841, to parents Cornelius and Margret. He lived in Scituate and worked as a fisherman. He enlisted on September 2, 1862. On September 12, 1862, he mustered into service for 9 months into the 43rd Regiment Mass. Volunteer Infantry, Company F. John mustered out July 30, 1863.

Claireborne Downs

Claireborne was 20 years old and worked as a laborer when he enlisted on October 11, 1864, for three years at Vicksburg, Mississippi. On October 17, 1864, he mustered in as a private in the 5th Colored Heavy Artillery, Company K. He mustered out on May 20, 1866. Claireborne was listed as part of the contraband soldiers added to the Scituate quota. He received a $125 bounty from the town.

Martin Dumphy

Martin was a 27 year-old tinsmith living in Scituate. He enlisted February 1, 1864, and mustered into service on February 4, 1864. He received a $125 bounty from the town. He served in the 59th Regiment Mass. Volunteer Infantry, Company E and was killed June 17, 1864, in Petersburg, Virginia.

William Jr. Dunbar

William was born in Hingham, MA to parents William and Sarah. He was married and lived in Scituate working as a shoemaker and ropemaker when he mustered into service on June 15, 1861, for three years in the 7th Regiment Mass. Volunteer Infantry, Company K. He was discharged for disability on March 17, 1862, at Washington, D.C. He re-enlisted June 16, 1862, for three years and mustered into service on August 9, 1862, as a private in the 35th Regiment Mass. Volunteer Infantry, Company A. He received $100 bounty from the town. William was wounded August 19, 1864, at Weldon Railroad, Virginia and died of his wounds on October 11, 1864, in a hospital in Alexandria, Virginia.

James Edson

James was born August 15, 1842, in Bridgewater, Massachusetts to Barnabus and Betsey. He was married and worked as a bootmaker. He mustered into service on July 20, 1864, for 100 days as a 5th sergeant in the 42nd Regiment Mass. Volunteer Infantry, Company D. He mustered out November 11, 1864.

James Horace Ellms

James Horace was born in Scituate April 14, 1841, to parents William and Caroline (Cook) Ellms. He worked as a mason. He mustered into service on December 22, 1863, for three years as a private in the 2nd Regiment Mass. Volunteer Heavy Artillery. James Horace died August 5, 1864, in a Portsmouth, Virginia hospital of typhoid fever.

Melzar James Elms

Melzar was born in Portsmouth, New Hampshire on March 24, 1846, to parents Noah and Abigail. He was a farmer residing in Worcester when he enlisted on August 16, 1863, for three years. Melzar mustered into service on October 8, 1863, as a private in the 2nd Regiment Mass. Volunteer Heavy Artillery, Company F. He mustered out of service July 6, 1865, in Company C.

Lou (Equie) Equq

Lou was residing in Springfield Massachusetts as a cook when he enlisted and mustered into service on December 7, 1864, in the 1st Regiment Mass. Volunteer Cavalry, Company H at the age of twenty-five. He received $125 bounty from the town and $115 from private funds. He was discharged May 30, 1865.

Charles Martin Ferguson

Charles was born in Scituate on August 16, 1843, to parents William and Lydia C.(Curtis) Ferguson. He was single and a farmer when he enlisted July 9, 1864, for 100 days and mustered into service on July 20, 1864, as a private in the 42nd Regiment Mass. Volunteer Infantry, Company D. Charles mustered out of service November 11, 1864.

Luke Grovener Fitts

Luke was born in Duxbury, February 14, 1832, to parents Luke and Lydia. He was married and residing in Scituate as a shoemaker when he was drafted and mustered into service for three years on September 18, 1863, as a private in the 32nd Regiment Mass. Volunteer Infantry, Company E. On May 12, 1864, Luke was wounded from a musket ball through his left hand at Laurel Hill, Virginia. He was discharged for his wounds on October 25, 1864.

Seth Otis Fitts

Seth was born in Pembroke on September 6, 1840, to parents Luke and Lydia. He was single and a shoemaker when he enlisted on August 19, 1862, for three years and mustered into service on August 20, 1862, as a private in the 38th Regiment Mass. Volunteer Infantry, Company K. He was wounded at Winchester, Virginia on September 19, 1864. He mustered out of service on July 12, 1865. He received a $100 bounty from the town.

Samuel Fouse

Samuel was residing as a miller in Scituate. He was twenty-nine years old when he enlisted April 2, 1864, and mustered into service for three years on April 12, 1864, as a private in the 5th Regiment Mass. Volunteer Cavalry, Company K. He was discharged July 8, 1864. He died of disease in Portsmouth, Virginia as a corporal. He had received a bounty of $125 from the town and $25 from private funds.

Warren Fuller

Warren was born in Watertown on October 4, 1835, to parents Ebenser and Lucinda. He was married and a shoemaker, machinist residing in Scituate when he enlisted and mustered into service on February 22, 1862, as a private in the 32nd Regiment Mass. Volunteer Infantry, Company F. He was wounded July 2, 1863, at the Battle of Gettysburg, Pennsylvania from a musket ball through the right foot. He was discharged with wounds August 24, 1863, in Boston.

Joy Kingsman Gannett

Joys' parents were Seth and Martha Ann T (James) Gannett. He was married and worked as a shoemaker. At the age of twenty, he enlisted and mustered into service on August 11, 1864, as a private in the 4th Regiment Mass. Volunteer Heavy Artillery, Company C. He served for one year and was discharged June 17, 1865. He received a bounty of $125 from the town and $75 from private funds.

Alvin Glines

Alvin was born on December 25, 1845, to parents Andrew and Cynthia. Alvin was single and working as a farmer when he enlisted for three years on August 11, 1862, and mustered into service September 2, 1862, as a private in the 39th Regiment Mass. Volunteer Infantry, Company G. He mustered out of service June 2, 1865.

Arudd Hamuer

Arudd is listed on town records as enlisting in the 1st Regiment Mass. Volunteer Cavalry. He received a bounty of $125 from the town and $115 from private funds.

John Harris

John was born in Cape Breton N.S. Canada on May 3, 1835, to parents John and Lucy Harris. He was married and worked as a fisherman. John mustered into service for three years on July 5, 1861, as a private in the 14th Regiment Mass. Volunteer Infantry, Company A. He mustered out on July 8, 1864.

George Anson Hatch

George was born on February 28, 1839, in Scituate to parents Turner and Elizabeth F. (Clapp) Hatch. He was married and working as a carpenter in Scituate when he enlisted September 2, 1862. On September 12, 1862, he mustered into service for nine months as a private in the 43rd Regiment Mass. Volunteer Infantry, Company F. He mustered out of service July 30, 1863. He received a $100 bounty from the town.

Charles Russell Hayes

Charles was born in Chelsea, Massachusetts on February 28, 1847, to parents Oliver P. and Mary T Hayes. He was single and working as a shoemaker when he enlisted and mustered into service August 11, 1864, as a private in the 4th Regiment Mass. Volunteer Heavy Artillery,

Company C. He received a $125 bounty from the town and $75 in private funds. He mustered out June 17, 1865.

Oliver Francis Hayes

Oliver was born on July 16, 1845, in Chelsea to parents Oliver P. and Mary T Hayes. Oliver was single and working as shoemaker and mechanic when he enlisted for three years and mustered into service on June 15, 1861, as a private in the 7th Regiment Mass. Volunteer Infantry, Company K. He mustered out of service June 27, 1864. Oliver re-enlisted and mustered into service for one year on April 7, 1865, in the 62nd Regiment Mass. Volunteer Infantry, Company A. He was promoted to corporal April 17, 1865, and mustered out of service May 5, 1865. He received a $125 bounty from the town.

Andrew Jackson Hobson

Andrew was born in Scituate on November 24, 1833, to parents Aaron and Sarah. He was married and working as a carpenter when he enlisted and mustered into service on August 10, 1864, as a private in the 4th Regiment Mass. Volunteer Heavy Artillery, Company C. He mustered out June 17, 1865.

George Washington Hodgdon

George was born in Eliot, Maine to Thomas Goodwin and Abigail. He was single and working as a mason in Scituate when he enlisted and mustered into service as a private on June 15, 1861, in the 7th Regiment Mass. Volunteer Infantry, Company K. He was transferred to the U.S. Navy on February 21, 1862. He served on the *USS Cincinnati* and *Lexington*. George was discharged September 25, 1863.

John Hughes

John was listed in the town records as a substitute for Henry Merritt. He received a bounty of $125 from the town and $225 in private funds.

William Webster Hunt

William was born on August 29, 1847, to parents Howland and Olivia. He was single and working as a shoemaker when he enlisted and mustered into service on August 10, 1864, as a private in the 4th Regiment Mass. Volunteer Heavy Artillery, Company C. He mustered out of service June 17, 1865. He received a bounty of $125 by the town and $75 in private funds.

Albert Hutchinson

Albert was born in Dorchester, Massachusetts on April 10, 1840, to parents Jesse D. and Patience (Vinal) Hutchinson. He was working as a mason when he enlisted on November 6, 1861, at Boston and mustered out on November 10, 1864, at Camp Woodbury, Virginia. He served three years with the U.S. Engineer Corps Artif., Company C.

Nelson Vinal Hutchinson

Nelson was born in Scituate on April 24, 1845, to parents Jesse D. and Sarah (Little) Hutchinson. He was single and working as a farmer when he enlisted as a private for three years and mustered into service on June 15, 1861, in the 7th Regiment Mass. Volunteer Infantry, Company K. He was promoted to corporal in April 1863, and wounded May 3, 1863, at the Battle of Fredericksburg, Virginia from a musket ball to the leg. He mustered out of service June 27, 1864.

Andrew M. Hyland

Andrew was born in Scituate on April 6, 1841, to parents Peleg and Mary Jane (Turner) Hyland. He was single and worked as a shoemaker. Andrew mustered into service for three years on August 20, 1862, as a private in the 38th Regiment Mass. Volunteer Infantry, Company D. Andrew died November 17, 1862, in Baltimore, Maryland of typhoid fever. He was sick for two weeks.

Edmund Lewis Hyland

Edmund was born in Scituate on December 16, 1843, to parents Edmund and Hannah (Wheelwright) Hyland. He was single and working as a shoemaker in Scituate when he enlisted and mustered into service for three years on February 22, 1862, as a private in the 32nd Regiment Mass. Volunteer Infantry, Company F. He re-enlisted on January 1, 1864. He mustered out of service June 29, 1865, as a corporal.

Edward James Hyland

Edward was born in Scituate on May 1, 1817, to parents Elisha and Lydia Young (Little) Hyland. He was married and working as a carpenter when he enlisted and mustered into service June 15, 1861, as a private in the 7th Regiment Mass. Volunteer Infantry, Company K. He was promoted to corporal in October 1861 and then sergeant in April 1863. Edward was wounded May 3, 1863, at the Battle of Fredericksburg, Virginia from a musket ball through the thigh. He was transferred to Veteran Reserve Corps January 22, 1864, and mustered out of service June 14, 1864.

Thomas Wilson Hyland

Thomas was born in Cohasset, Massachusetts on September 3, 1844, to parents Isaiah and Deborah (Studley) Hyland. He was single and worked as a shoemaker. Thomas enlisted on September 2, 1862, for nine months and mustered into service on September 12, 1862, as a private in the 43rd Regiment Mass. Volunteer Infantry, Company F. He received a bounty of $100 from the town and mustered out of service July 30, 1863.

Caleb Morton Jenkins

Caleb was born on July 27, 1823, to parents Caleb and Deborah (Foster) Jenkins. He was married and working as a shipwright when he enlisted on August 4, 1862. He mustered into service August 20, 1862, as a private in the 38th Regiment Mass. Volunteer Infantry, Company G. Caleb was discharged for disability on July 15, 1863, in New Orleans, Louisiana. He received a $100 bounty from the town.

Michael Johnson

Michael was 19 years old and worked as a laborer when he enlisted for three years on August 31, 1864, at Vicksburg, Mississippi. He received a $125 bounty from the town and he was listed as part of the contraband soldiers added to the Scituate quota. Michael served in the 72nd Illinois Regiment Volunteer Infantry.

Thomas Jones

Thomas was listed in the town records as serving in the 2nd Regiment Mass. Volunteer Infantry. He received $125 bounty from the town and $25 in private funds.

William Kerr

William was listed in the town records as a substitute for Alanson A. C. Gilbert. He received a $125 bounty from the town and $225 in private funds.

George Knighton

George was twenty-one years old residing in Scituate working as a seaman when he enlisted on January 27, 1864. He mustered into service February 25, 1864, as a private in the 56th Regiment Mass. Volunteer Infantry, Company K. He mustered out on July 12, 1865. He received a $125 bounty from the town.

Henry Watson Leavitt

Henry was born in South Scituate on December 24, 1847, to parents George W. and Emeline (Damon) Leavitt. He was single and working as a shoemaker when he enlisted and mustered into service on December 8, 1863, as a private in the 39th Regiment Mass. Volunteer Infantry, Company G. He was imprisoned August 19, 1864, at Weldon Railroad, VA and exchanged November 26, 1864. He transferred to the 32nd Regiment Mass. Infantry in June 2, 1865, and mustered out of service June 29, 1865.

Francis Bates Lee

Francis was born on November 3, 1843, to parents George C. and Olivia H. (Fisher) Lee. He was residing in Scituate and working as a carpenter when he enlisted and mustered into service on August 10, 1864, as a private in the 4th Regiment Heavy Artillery, Company C. He was discharged June 17, 1865.

George Washington Lee

George was born in Scituate on March 5, 1839, to parents Stephen and Catherine E. (Pratt) Lee. He was single and working as a shoemaker, machinist when he enlisted August 4, 1862. He mustered into service August 20, 1862, as a private in the 38th Regiment Mass. Volunteer Infantry, Company G. He received a $100 bounty from the town. George was promoted to corporal May 5, 1863, and was discharged for disability on November 6, 1863, in Boston.

Elwood Mozart Litchfield

Elwood was born in Scituate on May 8, 1847, to parents Sumner and Lillis (Litchfield). He worked as a farmer when he enlisted for one year and mustered into service on August 9, 1864, as a private in the 4th Regiment Mass. Volunteer Heavy Artillery, Company C. He was mustered out on June 17, 1865. He received a $125 bounty from the town and $75 in private funds.

Francis Henry Litchfield

Francis was born in Scituate on March 6, 1844, to parents Joseph and Jane (Whitcomb) Litchfield . He was single and working as a shoemaker and a farmer when he enlisted for three years. Francis mustered into service on June 15, 1861, as a private in the 7th Regiment Mass. Volunteer Infantry, Company K. He mustered out of service June 27, 1864.

Francis Mason Litchfield

Francis was born in Scituate on June 27, 1844, to parents Harvey and Betsey (Cushing) Litchfield. He was a single farmer when he enlisted for nine months and mustered into service on September 12, 1862, as a private in the 43rd Regiment Mass. Volunteer Infantry, Company F. He received a $100 bounty from the town and was discharged July 30, 1863.

Galen Litchfield

Galen was born in Watertown on June 22, 1839, to parents Issac and Priscilla (Litchfield). He was residing in Scituate working as a plumber and a farmer when he enlisted for three years and mustered into service on June 15, 1861, as a private in the 7th Regiment Mass. Volunteer Infantry, Company K. He was discharged January 17, 1863, for dysentery at a camp near Falmouth, Virginia.

Galen Watson Litchfield

Galen was born in Scituate on January 17, 1842, to parents Joseph and Jane (Whitcomb) Litchfield. He was single and working as a shoemaker, stitcher when he enlisted for three years and mustered into service on June 15, 1861, as a private in the 7th Regiment Mass. Volunteer Infantry, Company K. He mustered out of service June 27, 1864.

George Briggs Litchfield

George was born in Scituate on November 29, 1834, to parents Freeman and Lucy (Damon) Litchfield. He was married and working as a caulker and graver when he enlisted on February 24, 1862, as a private in the 32nd Regiment Mass. Volunteer Infantry, Company F. He was discharged for disability on February 9, 1863 in Alexandria, Virginia.

George Richmond Litchfield

George was born in Quincy, Massachusetts on April 19, 1848, to the parents of Richmond and Eliza (Richmond) Litchfield. He was single and working as a shoemaker and a farmer in Scituate when he enlisted and mustered into service on August 10, 1864, as a private in the 4th Regiment Mass. Volunteer Heavy Artillery, Company C. He mustered out June 17, 1865. He received a $125 bounty from the town and $75 from private funds.

Ira Litchfield

Ira was born January 20, 1834, in Scituate to parents Orange and Elizabeth (Merritt) Litchfield. He worked as a carpenter and was married. Ira mustered into service as a private on August 18, 1864, for one year in the 4th Regiment Mass. Volunteer Heavy Artillery, Company C. Ira mustered out on June 17, 1865. He received $125 from the town and $75 from private funds.

Milton Gray Litchfield

Milton was born in Scituate on March 10, 1844, to parents Summer and Lillis (Litchfield). He worked as a shoemaker and farmer when he enlisted on September 2, 1862. Milton mustered into service on September 12, 1862, for nine months in the 43rd Regiment Mass. Volunteer Infantry, Company F. He was mustered out on July 30, 1863. He received $100 bounty from the town. Milton re-enlisted and mustered into service on August 10, 1864, in the 4th Regiment Mass. Volunteer Heavy Artillery, Company C. He mustered out on June 17, 1865, as a corporal. He received $125 from the town and $75 from a private source.

Otis Litchfield

Otis was born on April 2, 1828, in Scituate to parents Daniel Jr. and Hannah (Litchfield). He worked as a farmer and was married. He enlisted on September 2, 1862, and mustered into service for nine months as a private in the 43rd Regiment Mass. Volunteer Infantry, Company, F. Otis mustered out of service on July 30, 1863. He received $100 bounty from the town.

Sumner Otis Litchfield

Sumner was born in Scituate on August 12, 1842, to parents Sumner and Lillis (Litchfield). He was single and working as a shoemaker when he enlisted on August 4, 1862, for three years. Sumner mustered into service on August 20, 1862, as a private in the 38th Regiment Mass. Volunteer Infantry, Company G. He was promoted to corporal on January 1, 1864, and wounded October 19, 1864, in Cedar Creek, Virginia by a shell fragment to the left leg. Sumner was discharged June 9, 1865, at Savannah, Georgia. He received a $100 bounty from the town.

Thomas Litchfield

Thomas was born on September 23, 1824, to parents Thomas and Mabel (Vinal) Litchfield. He was residing in Scituate, married, and working as a carpenter when he enlisted for one year and mustered into service on August 10, 1864, as a private in the 4th Regiment Mass. Volunteer Heavy Artillery, Company C. Thomas mustered out June 17, 1865. He received a $125 bounty from the town and $75 in private funds.

Warren Jr. Litchfield

Warren was born on February 27, 1844, in Scituate to parents Warren and Helen (Litchfield). He worked as a farmer and enlisted on September 2, 1862. He received $100 bounty from the town. Warren mustered into service for nine months as a private in the 43rd Regiment Mass. Volunteer Infantry, Company F. He died on June 27, 1863, at Foster General Hospital in Newbern, North Carolina of typhoid fever. He had been sick for three weeks.

Warren Studley Litchfield

Warren was born in Scituate on October 26, 1844, to parents Samuel and Cordelia (Studley) Litchfield. He was single and working as a farmer and a shoemaker when he enlisted on August 4, 1862. He mustered into service on August 20, 1862, as a private in the 38th Regiment Mass. Volunteer Infantry, Company G. He received a $100 bounty from the town. Warren died in Baton Rouge, Louisiana from disease on September 4, 1863.

William Litchfield

William was born in Scituate on February 25, 1826, to parents Meshech and Temperance (Stoddard) Litchfield. He was married and working as a shoemaker when he enlisted on February 24, 1862, as a private in the 32nd Regiment Mass. Volunteer Infantry, Company F. He mustered out of service April 19, 1865.

William Litchfield

William was born in Watertown on August 16, 1842, to parents Issac and Priscilla (Litchfield). He was single and residing in Scituate working as a blacksmith when he enlisted for three years and mustered into service on June 15, 1861, as a private in the 7th Regiment Mass. Volunteer Infantry, Company K. He was promoted to corporal on April 24, 1863, and mustered out of service on June 27, 1864.

William Gertrude Litchfield

William was born in Scituate on March 12, 1840, to parents Joseph and Jane (Whitcomb) Litchfield. He was single and working as a shoemaker, shoe cutter when he enlisted for three years and mustered into service on June 15, 1861, as a private in the 7th Regiment Mass. Volunteer Infantry, Company K. He was discharged September 29, 1863, for disability at Culpepper, Virginia.

Michael Maddigan

Michael was twenty-three years old and working as a laborer when he enlisted and mustered into service on December 13, 1864, as a private in the 11th Battery Mass. Volunteer Light Artillery. He was discharged June 16, 1865. He received a $125 bounty from the town and $50 in private funds.

Charles Dexter Mann

Charles was born in Scituate on November 17, 1838, to parents Charles and Mary D. (Lothrop) Mann. He was married and working as a farmer when he enlisted on September 2, 1862. Charles mustered into service on September 12, 1862, as a private in the 43rd Regiment Mass. Volunteer Infantry, Company F. He was discharged October 24, 1862, at Boston, Massachusetts on a surgeon's certificate of disability.

Thomas Eliot Mann

Thomas was born in Boston on November 8, 1820, to parents Isaiah and Hannah. He was residing in Scituate working as a farmer when he mustered into service on October 9, 1862, as a private in the 47th Regiment Mass. Volunteer Infantry, Company F. He mustered out of service on September 1, 1863.

Joseph Owen Marsh

Joseph was born in Scituate on October 22, 1843, to parents John and Lucy (Dunbar) Marsh. He was single and working as a shoemaker, mechanic when he enlisted for three years and mustered into service as a private on June 15, 1861, in the 7th Regiment Mass. Volunteer Infantry, Company K. He mustered out of service June 27, 1864.

Christopher McAndrew

Christopher McAndrew was residing in Providence, Rhode Island at the age of twenty-five working as a laborer when he enlisted and mustered into service on December 13, 1864, as a private in the 11th Battery Mass. Volunteer Light Artillery. He received a $125 bounty from the town and $50 in private funds.

Dennis McCarthy

Dennis was born in Ireland. His father's name was Jeremiah. He was residing in Scituate working as a tailor when he enlisted on February 27, 1864, and mustered into service on March 4, 1864, as a private in the 59th Regiment Mass. Volunteer Infantry. He was discharged July 31, 1865, and received $125 bounty from the town and $25 in private funds.

Michael McGill

Michael was listed in the town records as enlisting in the 15th Regiment Mass. Volunteer Heavy Artillery. He received $125 bounty from the town and $100 in private funds.

Benjamin Franklin Merritt

Benjamin was born in Scituate on October 24, 1821, to parents Ensign and Sally (Cook) Merritt. He was married and worked as a master mariner. Benjamin enlisted for three years and mustered into service on August 20, 1862, as a private in the 39th Regiment Mass. Volunteer Infantry, Company C. He was discharged on August 21, 1863, from a disability in Washington D.C. He received a $100 bounty from the town.

Billings Merritt

Billings was born in Scituate on September 24, 1830, to parents Martin and Debby (Bailey) Merritt. He was married and living in Scituate working as a carpenter when he enlisted on August 15, 1862. Billings mustered into service on August 20, 1862, as a private in the 38th Regiment Mass. Volunteer Infantry, Company D. He received a $200 bounty from the town of Hingham. He mustered out of service on June 30, 1864, as a sergeant.

Edmond Francis Merritt

Edmond was born in Scituate on October 17, 1846, to parents Munroe and Harriet (Litchfield) Merritt. He worked as a shoemaker. Edmond enlisted and mustered into service on August 10, 1864, as a private in the 4th Regiment Mass. Volunteer Heavy Artillery, Company C. He mustered out of service on June 17, 1865. He received a $125 bounty from the town and $75 from private funds.

George Merritt

George was born in Scituate on February 4, 1834, to parents Shadrach B. and Arvilla (Litchfield) Merritt. He was married and worked as a carpenter. George enlisted and mustered into service on August 16, 1864, as an artificer in the 4th Regiment Mass. Volunteer Heavy Artillery, Company C. He mustered out of service on June 17, 1865. He received a $125 bounty from the town and $75 from private funds

George Whitney Merritt

George was born in Scituate on October 6, 1831, to parents Dexter and Abigail B. (Merritt). He was married and working as a farmer when he enlisted on August 4, 1862. George mustered into service on August 20, 1862, as a private in the 38th Regiment Mass. Volunteer Infantry, Company G. He received a $100 bounty from the town. He was promoted to corporal in October 1862, and sergeant on March 1, 1863. He was discharged for disability on August 13, 1863, in New Orleans as a sergeant. George re-enlisted on July 9, 1864, and mustered into the 4th Regiment Mass. Volunteer Heavy Artillery, Company C. He received $125 bounty and $75 in private funds. George was promoted to 1st lieutenant on August 16, 1864. He mustered out June 17, 1865.

Harvey Merritt

Harvey was born in Scituate on July 16, 1826, to parents James L. and Emily (Litchfield) Merritt. He was married and worked as a blacksmith. Harvey enlisted and mustered into service on August 10, 1864, as an artificer in the 4th Regiment Mass. Volunteer Heavy Artillery, Company C. He mustered out of service on June 17, 1865. He received a $125 bounty from the town and $75 from private funds.

Munroe Merritt

Munroe was born in Scituate on August 27, 1820, to parents James L. and Emily (Litchfield) Merritt. He was married and worked as a shoemaker. Munroe enlisted and mustered into service on August 16, 1864, as a private in the 4th Regiment Mass. Volunteer Heavy Artillery, Company C. He mustered out of service on June 17, 1865. He received a $125 bounty from the town and $75 from private funds.

William Otis Merritt

William was born in Scituate on November 29, 1822, to parents Billings and Abigail (Brooks) Merritt. He was married and working as a farmer when he enlisted for three years and mustered into service on June 15, 1861, as a private in the 7th Regiment Mass. Volunteer Infantry, Company K. He was discharged August 25, 1863, for dysentery after spending seven months at a camp near Warrenton, Virginia.

William Otis Merritt, Jr.

William was born on September 1, 1844, to parents William O. and Joanna (Merritt). He worked as a caulker. William enlisted on

September 2, 1862, and mustered into service on September 12, 1862, in the 43rd Regiment Mass. Volunteers Infantry, Company F. He received $100 bounty from the town. He was discharged on July 30, 1863. William re-enlisted and mustered into service as a corporal on August 15, 1864, in the 4th Regiment Mass. Volunteer Heavy Artillery, Company C. He was promoted to sergeant on May 13, 1865, and was discharged on June 17, 1865. He received a $125 bounty from the town and $75 from private funds.

John Mitchell

John was twenty-four years old working as a farmer when he enlisted on January 26, 1864, and mustered into service on February 8, 1864, as a private in the 4th Regiment Mass. Volunteer Cavalry, Company B. He received a $125 bounty from the town.

John Moore

John was living in Boston working as a boatman. At the age of twenty-four, he enlisted and mustered into service on May 18, 1864, as a private in the 2nd Regiment Mass. Volunteer Infantry. He received a $125 bounty from the town and $25 in private funds.

Gilman F. Morrill

Gilman was working as a carpenter. At the age of forty-one, he enlisted and mustered into service on March 25, 1864, as a private in the 40th Regiment Mass. Volunteer Infantry. He received a $125 bounty from the town and $25 in private funds.

Joseph Warren Morris

Joseph was born in Scituate on October 5, 1828, to parents William and Rebekah (Colborn) Morris. He was married and working as a shoe manufacturer when he enlisted on September 2, 1862. Joseph mustered into service on September 12, 1862, as a private in the 43rd Regiment Mass. Volunteer Infantry, Company F. He mustered out of service on July 30, 1863. He received a $100 bounty from the town.

John Murphy

John was living in New Haven, Connecticut and working as a boat builder. At age 18 he enlisted and mustered into service on June 14, 1860, in the 1st Regiment Mass. Volunteer Heavy Artillery, Company

C. He furloughed from the hospital November 4, 1860 and return to his regiment. He received $125 bounty from the town and $50 in private funds.

Thomas Murphy

Thomas was living in Boston working as a laborer. At the age of twenty-two, he enlisted and mustered into service on May 18, 1864, in the 2nd Regiment Mass. Volunteer Infantry. He received $125 bounty from the town and $25 in private funds.

Thomas Nash

Thomas was born in Lowell, Massachusetts on July 5, 1838, to parents Lemuel and Mary. He was single and working as a farmer when he mustered into service on October 9, 1862, as a private in the 47th Mass. Volunteer Infantry, Company F. He received a $200 bounty in Boston and mustered out on September 1, 1863.

John Briggs Newcomb

John was born in Scituate on November 27, 1840, to parents Levi and Joan (Studley) Newcomb. He was single and working as a shoemaker when he enlisted and mustered into to service on June 15, 1861, as a private in the 7th Mass. Volunteer Infantry, Company K. He suffered from wounds from a musket ball on May 3, 1863, at the Battle of Fredericksburg, Virginia. He died on May 7, 1863, at Potomac Creek Hospital from wounds received in action.

Thomas Jefferson Newcomb

Thomas was born in Scituate on August 18, 1840, to parents Jacob and Roxanna (Vinal) Newcomb. He was single and residing in Scituate working as a shoemaker when he enlisted and mustered into service for three years on October 19, 1861, as a private in the 24th Regiment Mass. Volunteer Infantry, Company F. He was discharged for disability on January 16, 1864, in Beaufort, South Carolina.

Elias Oliver Nichols

Elias was born in Scituate on April 1, 1839, to parents Benjamin and Sophronia (Pincin) Nichols. He worked as a blacksmith. Elias enlisted on August 4, 1862, for three years and mustered into service as a private on August 20, 1862, in the 38th Regiment Mass Volunteer Infantry, Company G. He was taken prisoner at Battle of Cedar Creek on October

19, 1864, and was sent to Salisbury, North Carolina as a corporal on November 4, 1864. There is no further record. He had received a $100 bounty from the town.

Asahel Foster Nott

Asahel was born in Scituate on May 22, 1830, to parents Asahel and Delilah (Studley) Nott. He was married and working as a shoemaker when he enlisted and mustered into service on June 15, 1861, as a private in the 7th Regiment Mass. Volunteer Infantry, Company K. He was discharged December 3, 1862, on a Surgeon's Certificate for disability at Brooklyn, NY. Asahel was drafted July 21, 1863, and mustered into service as a private September 18, 1863, in the 32nd Regiment Mass. Volunteer Infantry, Company E. He was wounded in the arm May 7, 1864, at Wilderness, Virginia and mustered out of service June 12, 1865.

Charles Henry Nott

Charles was born on April 3, 1839, to parents Asahel and Delilah (Studley) Nott. He was single and working as a shoemaker when he enlisted for three years and mustered into service on June 15, 1861, as a private in the 7th Regiment Mass. Volunteer Infantry, Company K. He mustered out of service June 27, 1864.

Hosea Dunbar Nott

Hosea was born on October 3, 1838, to parents Asahel and Delilah (Studley) Nott. He was residing in Scituate as a single shoemaker when he enlisted for three years and mustered into service on June 15, 1861, as a private in the 7th Regiment Mass. Volunteer Infantry, Company K. He was discharged January 4, 1863, for disability from a Surgeon's certificate of disability at a camp near Falmouth, Virginia.

Daniel O'Connor

Daniel O'Connor was twenty-nine when he enlisted and mustered into service on January 30, 1864, as a private in the 3rd Regiment Mass. Volunteer Cavalry. He received a $125 bounty from the town.

William Hyland Osborn(e)

William was born in Scituate on December 22, 1840, to parents Caleb and Mary A. (Hyland) Osborne. He was working as a shoemaker when he enlisted and mustered into service on December 2, 1861, as a private in the 32nd Regiment Mass. Volunteer Infantry, Company E. He was wounded on July 2, 1863, in the Battle of Gettysburg, PA when a shell fragment hit his knee. He was transferred to the Veteran Reserve Corps (V.R.C.), March 15, 1864, and mustered out December 16, 1864. William Hyland Osborn(e) was a charter member and served as Post Commander of the local chapter of the Grand Army of the Republic (G.A.R.), George W. Perry Post No. 31.

James Edwin Otis

James was born in Scituate on April 11, 1842, to parents Edwin and Margaret A. (Brown) Otis. He was working as a farmer when he enlisted on July 9, 1864, and mustered into service on July 22, 1864, as a private in the 42nd Regiment Mass Volunteer Infantry, Company D. He mustered out of service on November 11, 1864.

Thomas Otis

Thomas was born in Scituate on January 24, 1842, to parents Joseph and Sarah N. (Jackman) Otis. He was married and residing in Scituate working as a shoemaker when he enlisted and mustered into service on August 10, 1864, as a private in the 4th Regiment Mass. Volunteer Heavy Artillery, Company C. He mustered out of service on June 17, 1865.

John Paltong

John was twenty-eight years old and worked as a harness maker. John enlisted and mustered in as a private on February 2, 1864, in the 3rd Regiment Mass. Volunteer Cavalry, Company I. He died of disease June 8, 1865, in Cumberland Maryland. He received a $125 bounty from the town.

John Briggs Peirce

John was born in Scituate July 22, 1832, to parents Nathaniel and Sophia (Briggs) Peirce. He was married and working as a mason when he enlisted and mustered into service on August 10, 1864, as a private in the 4th Regiment Mass. Volunteer Heavy Artillery, Company C. He mustered out of service June 17, 1865.

George Leonard Perry

George L. Perry was born in Quincy Mass on March 9, 1846 to Leonard and Harriet (Manley) Perry. He worked as a farmer and, at the age of 18, he enlisted and mustered into service on August 10, 1864, in the 4th

Battalion Mass. Volunteer Heavy Artillery Company C for one year. He was mustered out on June 17, 1865 at Washington D.C.

George Whitmarsh Perry

George was born in Scituate on December 15, 1846, to parents Samuel and Eliza (Bryant) Perry. He was single and working as a farmer and a shoemaker when he enlisted on September 2, 1862. George mustered into service on September 12, 1862, as a private for nine months in the 43rd Regiment Mass. Volunteer Infantry, Company F. He received a $100 bounty from the town. He mustered out July 30, 1863. George re-enlisted March 17, 1864, as a private in the 58th Regiment Mass. Volunteer Infantry, Company I. He was promoted to sergeant. George was taken prisoner September 30, 1864, at the Battle on Weldon Railroad. On January 13, 1865, he died of disease at Salisbury Prison in North Carolina. The Grand Army of the Republic Post No. 31 in Scituate was named in his honor.

Ethan A.S. Pool

Ethan A.S. Pool, a shoemaker, served as a seaman on The *Ohio*, USS *Ticonderoga*, and *Conemaugh* and he was discharged December 15, 1864.

Rufus W. Porter

Rufus Porter was born in 1839 in Warren NH. At the age of 25, and working as a farmer, he enlisted as a private for one year on January 25, 1864. He was mustered into service on February 5, 1864, into the 56th Regiment Mass. Volunteer Infantry, Company I. He was paid a bounty of $125 by the Town. Wounded in the Battle of the Wilderness on May 6, 1864, he was transferred to the Veteran's Reserve Corp. on April 1, 1865, and mustered out on August 23, 1865, from the 39th Battalion Veteran's Reserve Corps. He also served in the 3rd VT. Infantry Company G.

Michael Portley

Michael Portley enlisted as a private on May 18, 1864, at the age of 26. At this time he was working as a shoemaker. He was mustered into service, on May 30, 1864, in the 3rd Regiment Mass. Volunteer Heavy Artillery, Company C for three years. He was commissioned

2nd Lieutenant on September 27, 1865, and was mustered out on September 18, 1865, as a 1st lieutenant.

Bardine Augusta Prouty

Bardine Prouty was born in Hingham on June 18, 1844, to Bardine H. and Esther (Brown) Prouty. He worked as a teamster and was living in Cohasset when, at the age of 18, he enlisted and was mustered on March 10, 1862, as a private for three years in the 1st Battalion Heavy Artillery Company A. He mustered out on March 25, 1864, and reenlisted the same day. He was paid a bounty of $100 by the town. He transferred to the 1st Battalion Mass. Heavy Artillery and mustered out October 20, 1864. He reenlisted and was paid $125 by the Town. He was wounded in the Battle of the Wilderness on May 5, 1864, receiving a musket ball through the right foot. He was mustered out October 20, 1865. He was a charter member of Post. 31 GAR.

Bardine Hyland Prouty

Bardine Hyland Prouty was born in Hingham on November 9, 1822 to Nathaniel and Matilda B. (Gregory) Prouty. He was a cook, living in Cohasset, when, at age 18, he enlisted and mustered on March 6, 1862, as a private for 3 years in the First Battalion Mass. Volunteer Heavy Artillery, Company A. He mustered out March 5, 1865. He was a Charter Member of Post 31, serving as Post Commander.

James Little Prouty

James Young Prouty was born in Scituate on June 20, 1843, to Caleb W. and Abigail Y. (Jenkins) Prouty. He was working as a clerk when he enlisted on July 9, 1864, at age 21. He mustered into service on July 21, 1864, in the 42nd Regiment Mass. Volunteer Infantry Company D as a corporal. He mustered out November 11, 1864. He was a member of GAR Post 31.

John Ensign Otis Prouty

John Prouty, James' brother, was born in Scituate on March 8, 1840, to Caleb and Abigail Young (Jenkins) Prouty. He worked as a fisherman. At the age of 22, he enlisted, on September 2, 1862, and was mustered into service on the September 12, 1862 as a private for nine months in the 43rd Regiment Mass. Volunteer Infantry, Company F. He was paid a $100 bounty. He was promoted to corporal on November 10, 1862, and was mustered out on July 20, 1863. He reenlisted on July 9, 1864 for 100 days and mustered on July 30, 1864, into the 42nd Regiment Mass. Volunteer Infantry, Company D. (The same day he was drafted.) He was mustered out the November 11, 1864. After the war he represented his district in the Legislature. He was a member of Post 31 serving as Post Commander. He also served as the keeper at the Scituate Lighthouse.

George W. Rich

George Rich was born in Scituate on February 5, 1837, to Moses Parker and Mary (Young) Rich. He was a farmer/clerk. At age 24 he enlisted and was mustered into service on June 15, 1861, as a private for three years in the 7th Regiment Mass. Regular Infantry Company K. He mustered out June 27, 1864, at Taunton, Massachusetts.

Elias H. Richardson

Elias Richardson was born in Haverhill in 1843 to C. C. and Eliza Richardson. He was a sailor. He enlisted and was mustered into service at the age of 21, on March 22, 1864, as a private for three years in the 28th Regiment Mass. Volunteer Infantry, Company C. He received a bounty of $125 from the Town and a $25 private donation. He was wounded on March 25, 1865, at Hatcher's Run Virginia and died of his wounds on May 2, 1865, at Washington D.C.

Marshall Peleg Ro[d]gers

Marshall Rogers was born in Marshfield on July 5, 1840, to Nathan and Betsey (Ayers) Rogers. He worked as a carpenter, and lived in Scituate, when he enlisted and mustered into service for three years on February 14, 1862, as an Artificer in the 3rd Rhode Island Heavy Artillery, Company A. He was 21. He was mustered out on the February 14, 1865 at Hilton Head, South Carolina.

Nathan Andrew Ro[d]gers

Nathan Rogers, the older brother of Marshall, was born in Marshfield to Nathan and Betsey (Ayers) Rogers on October 23, 1837. He was living in Scituate and working as a carpenter when, at the age of 24, he enlisted and mustered into service on June 26, 1861, in the 12th Regiment Mass. Volunteer Infantry, Company B as a private for three years. He was wounded on September 17, 1862, at the Battle of Antietam, Maryland. His left arm was shattered. He died at Patent Office Hospital in Washington, D.C. on November 13, 1862, of his wounds.

George W. Rowe

George Rowe of Lynn, Massachusetts was 29, and a farmer when he enlisted on April 15, 1861, for three years. He mustered into service April 30, 1861, into the 8th Regiment Mass. Volunteer Infantry, Company F. He mustered out on August 1, 1861. He was living in Lynn and working as a shoemaker when he reenlisted on September 1, 1862, and mustered on the 19th, as a sergeant in the 8th Regiment Mass. Volunteer Infantry, Company F. He mustered out on August 7, 1863. He re-enlisted and mustered a third time on August 18, 1864, in the 4th Regiment Mass. Volunteer Heavy Artillery Volunteer Infantry and received a bounty from the Town of $125. He mustered out on June 17, 1865.

Robert Sayles

Robert Sayles was 33 years of age from Scituate and a laborer when he enlisted on January 7, 1864. He was mustered on January 29, 1864, as a private for three years into the 5th Regiment Cavalry, Company B, receiving a bounty of $125 from the town. He mustered out on October 31, 1865, in Clarksville TX.

John (Johan) Schuknecht

John Schuknecht was 28 years of age from Boston, working as a sailor, when he enlisted and was mustered into service March 24, 1864, for three years in the 19th Regiment Mass. Volunteer Infantry, Company C. He received a bounty of $125 from the Town. On April 13, 1864 he applied for a transfer to the Navy. No further information is available,

Charles Parker Seaverns

Charles Seaverns was born in Dorchester on January 27, 1835, to Charles H. and Sarah L. Seaverns. At the age of 29, while working as a sailor, he enlisted and was mustered on August 9, 1864, in the 4th Regiment Mass. Volunteer Heavy Artillery, Company C. He was paid a bounty of $125 by the Town, and $75 privately. He was wounded in the Battle of Salem Church May 3, 1863, and transferred to a field hospital. He was transferred to several different hospitals and was mustered out on June 17, 1865, at Washington, D.C. After the war he represented his district in the Legislature and joined Post 31 G.A.R. serving as Adjutant and Commander.

Warren Hobart Sherman

Warren Sherman was born in Scituate February 27, 1841, to Israel and Clarissa (Stetson) Sherman. He was working as a blacksmith when he enlisted, at the age of 21, on September 2, 1862. He mustered September 1862 as a private for nine months in the 43rd Mass. Volunteer Infantry, Company F. He mustered out on July 30, 1863.

Michael Shine

Michael Shine was 30 years of age, from Providence R.I. working as a laborer, when he enlisted and was mustered on December 13, 1864, as a private for one year in the 11th Battery Mass. Volunteer Light Artillery. He was paid a bounty of $125 by the Town and $50 privately. He mustered out on June 16,1865.

Charles Henry Smith

Charles Smith was born June 10, 1840, in Cohasset to Thomas and Maria (Lawrence) Smith. He was working as a shoemaker and living in Scituate when he enlisted, at age 25, on July 9, 1864, as a corporal and mustered on July 20 for 100 days in the 42nd Regiment Mass. Volunteer Infantry, Company D. He mustered out of the service on November 11, 1864.

Charles William Soule

Charles was born in Abington on February 23, 1834, to Josiah and Sophronia Soule. He was living in Scituate when he married Anna E. Manson. He was 36 and working as a merchant/trader, when he enlisted and mustered on September 2, 1862, and mustered on September 12, 1862 as a private in the 43rd Infantry Regiment, Company F and was commissioned as a Sergeant. He mustered out on July 30, 1863 at Readville, Massachusetts.

Benjamin Elbridge Stetson

Benjamin Stetson was born in Scituate on April 28, 1844, to Peleg and Rachel Stetson. He was working as a laborer when he enlisted on August 4, 1862, at the age of 19. He mustered on August 20, 1862, in the 38th Regiment Mass. Volunteer Infantry, Company G. He was paid a bounty of $100 by the town. He was wounded in the finger on March 27, 1863, at the Battle of Port Hudson L.A. He mustered out on June 30, 1865.

Charles Cole Stetson

Charles Stetson was born in Scituate on May 17, 1846, to Peleg and Rachel Stetson, a younger brother to Benjamin. He was working as a mason when he enlisted at the age of 19, on July 9, 1864. He mustered as a private on July 20, 1864, in the 42nd Regiment Mass. Volunteer Infantry, Company D for 100 days. He was mustered out November 11, 1864.

Thomas Stone

Thomas Stone was living in New York and working as a clerk, when, at age 21, he enlisted and mustered on 24 March 1864, for three years in the 19th Regiment Mass. Volunteer Infantry, Company C. He received a bounty from the town of $125 and a $25 private donation. He was taken prisoner on June 22, 1864, near Petersburg Virginia. He was released on December 1, 1864, and mustered out on June 30, 1865.

Alfred Homer Studley

Alfred Studley was born in Scituate on January 22, 1842, to Homer and Lydia (Jenkins) Studley. He was working as a shoemaker when he enlisted, at the age of 20, on September 2, 1862. He mustered as a private on the 12th in the 43rd Regiment Mass. Volunteer Infantry, Company F. He received a bounty of $100 from the town. He mustered out on October 24, 1862, in Boston with a disability.

Edwin Studley

Edwin Studley was born in Scituate on May 7, 1835, to Lewis and Emily S. (Vinal) Studley. He was working as a sailor, when, at the age of 29, he enlisted on September 2, 1862. He mustered on September 12, 1862, in the 43rd Regiment Mass. Volunteer Infantry. He re-enlisted on the 9th of August 1864, as a private for one year in the 4th Regiment Mass. Volunteer Heavy Artillery, Company C. He mustered out on June 17, 1864 as a corporal in Washington, D.C. He was a charter member of Post 31 G.A.R. and is buried in Groveland Cemetery.

Horace Lincoln Studley

Horace Studey, a brother to Alfred was born in Scituate on September 14, 1837, to Homer and Lydia (Jenkins) Studley. He was working as a carpenter and living in Hingham, when, at the age of 24, he enlisted on December 2, 1861. He mustered the same day as a private for three years in the 38th Regiment Mass. Volunteer Infantry, Company E. He died in Hingham on April 1, 1863 of disease.

John Studley

John Studley, brother to Horace and Alfred, was born in Scituate on January 31, 1840, to Homer and Lydia Jenkins Studley. He was working as a mason when he enlisted on August 15, 1862, at the age of 22. He mustered as a private for 3 years into the 38th Regiment Mass. Volunteer Infantry, Company D on August 20, 1862. He received a bounty of $200 paid by the town of Hingham. He was promoted to corporal on April 28, 1864, he mustered out on July 30, 1865, at Savannah, GA.

Charles Franklin Sylvester

Charles Sylvester was born in Scituate on July 22, 1834, to Abel Jr. and Arabella (Vinal) Sylvester. He worked as a mechanic when he enlisted and mustered, at the age of 18, on June 15, 1861, in the 7th Regiment Mass. Volunteer Infantry, Company K. He mustered out July 30, 1864, at Taunton Massachusetts. He re-enlisted on August 9, 1864, and mustered the same day in the 4th Regiment Mass. Volunteer Heavy Artillery. He mustered out on June 27, 1865.

Edmond Howard Sylvester

Edmond Sylvester, a brother to Charles, was born in Hingham on October 25, 1834, to Abel Jr. and Arabella (Vinal) Sylvester. He was working as a mason and living in Scituate, when, at the age 26, he enlisted and mustered on June 15, 1861, as a private for 3 years in the 7th Regiment Mass. Volunteer Infantry, Company K. He was promoted to a full corporal on February 21, 1862. He was wounded on June 25, 1862, in the Battle of Fredericksburg Virginia, by a musket ball in the shoulder blade. He was transferred to the Veteran's Reserve Corp on June 15, 1864, and mustered out on June 16, 1864, as of Company K Veteran's Reserve Corps.

Gideon Young Sylvester

Gideon Sylvester was born in Scituate in April 1826, to James and Elizabeth (Young) Sylvester. He was worked as a shoemaker, when, at the age of 38, he enlisted on September 2, 1862. He mustered on September 12, 1862, in the 43rd Regiment Mass. Volunteer Infantry, Company F as a corporal for 9 months. He was transferred to Company B by the order of Colonel Holbrook. He was paid a bounty of $100 by the town, and was mustered out July 30, 1863. He reenlisted on August 9, 1864, and was mustered the same day as a corporal for 1 year in the 4th Regiment Heavy Artillery, Company C. He received a bounty of $125 from the town and $75 from a private donation. He was mustered out on June 17, 1865, at Washington D.C.

Charles Augustus Taylor

Charles Taylor was born in Boston on April 30, 1843, to John Stubbs and Cordelia (Alvard) Taylor. He was working as a fisherman and shoemaker when he enlisted, at age 19, in Scituate on August 18, 1862. He mustered two days later in the 38th Regiment Mass. Volunteer Infantry, Company G as a private for 3 years. He received a bounty of $100 from the Town. He was discharged for disability on February 16, 1864, at Baton Rouge, Louisiana.

Lucius Thayer

Lucius Thayer was born in Boston, living in Scituate, and working as a blacksmith when he enlisted on September 2, 1862, at the age of 32. Mustered 10 days later as a private for 3 years in the 43rd Regiment Mass. Volunteer Infantry, Company F. He received a bounty of $100 from the town. He mustered out on July 30, 1863.

Joseph Wyman Tilden

Joseph Tilden was born in Boston on February 25, 1813, to Joseph and Sally (Perkins) Tilden. He was living in Scituate and working as a farmer, when, at the age of 44, he enlisted and was mustered on August 10, 1864, as a Commissary Sergeant for 1 year in the 4th Regiment Mass. Volunteer Heavy Artillery, Company C. He was paid a bounty of $125 by the town, and $75 by private donation. He mustered out on June 17, 1865, in Washington D.C. as a Sergeant. He was a member of Post 31 G.A.R. serving as Quartermaster. He died in 1890 and is buried in Fairview Cemetery.

John Tirrell

John Tirrell was born in Goffstown, New Hampshire to Johnson and Abigail Tirrell. He lived in Scituate, and worked as a farmer/clerk when, at the age of 22, he was drafted and mustered on September 14, 1863, as a private for 3 years in the 32nd Regiment Mass. Volunteer Infantry, Company E. He was killed in the Battle of Petersburg, VA on June 18, 1864. He was shot through the heart.

David Otis Totman

David Totman was born in Scituate on September 20, 1832, to Benjamin and Eunice (Otis) Totman. He was working as a grain peddler when he enlisted, at the age of 30, on August 19, 1862. Mustered the next day for 3 years into the 38th Regiment Mass. Volunteer Infantry, Company G as a private. He received a bounty of $100 from the town. He was promoted corporal on March 1, 1863, and died April 18, 1863, at Baton Rouge, Louisiana of intermittent fever and heart disease.

John Henry Turner

John Turner was born in Scituate on February 7, 1835, to Perez and Sara (Pincin) Turner. He was working as a cordwainer (shoemaker) when he enlisted on September 2, 1862, at the age of 34. He mustered on September 12, 1862, in the 43rd Regiment Mass. Volunteer Infantry, Company F for nine months as a private. He was paid $100 bounty by the town and was mustered out on July 30, 1863. He was a member of Post 31 G.A.R.

Franklin Tyler

Franklin Tyler was born in New York on January 7, 1826, to Miles and Sally Tyler. He was living in Scituate and working as a farmer when he enlisted on September 2, 1862, as a private for nine months. He was mustered at the age of 30, on September 12, 1862, in the 43rd Regiment Mass. Volunteer Infantry, Company F. He received a bounty of $100 from the town. He was discharged on July 30, 1863.

Fenton Watson Varney

Fenton Varney was born in Scituate on November 1, 1844, to Nathaniel and Sophronia (Litchfield) Varney. He was 19 and worked as a shoemaker (as did his father) when he enlisted and mustered on August

10, 1864, as a private for one year in the 4th Regiment Mass. Volunteer Heavy Artillery, Company C. He received a bounty of $100 from the town. He was mustered out on June 17, 1865, at Washington D.C.

Allen L. Vinal

Allen Vinal was born in Scituate on July 21, 1831, to John and Abigail (Collier) Vinal. He was 34 and worked as a shoemaker when he enlisted and mustered on August 10, 1864, as a private for 1 year. He joined the 4th Regiment Mass. Volunteer Heavy Artillery, Company C and received a bounty of $175 from the Town and $75 from a private donation. He mustered out on June 17, 1864 at Washington, D.C

Charles Augustus Vinal

Charles Vinal was born in Scituate on March 23, 1843, to Freeman and Sarah A.M. (Green) Vinal. He was living in Cohasset and working as a farmer when he enlisted, at age 19, on September 2, 1862. He mustered on September 12, 1862, into the 43rd Regiment Mass. Volunteer Infantry, Company F as a private for nine months. He received a bounty of $100 from the town. He mustered out on July 7, 1863.

George Otis Vinal

George Vinal was born in Scituate on December 13, 1832, to Paul and Maria (Doane) Vinal. He was a shoemaker when he enlisted, the age of 29, on September 2, 1862, as a private for nine months. He mustered on September 12, 1862, in the 43rd Regiment Mass. Volunteer Infantry, Company F. He mustered out on July 30, 1863. He reenlisted and mustered on August 10, 1864, in the 4th Regiment Mass. Volunteer Heavy Artillery, Company C for one year. He received a bounty of $125 from the Town and $75 from a private donation and was mustered out on June 17, 1865, at Washington D.C. He was a charter member of Post 31 G.A.R.

Lucius Henry Vinal

Lucius Vinal (or Henry L. Vinal as he was known when he enlisted) was born in Scituate on February 23, 1833, to Charles and Elizabeth K. (Beal) Vinal. He was 31 when he enlisted as a private for 100 days on July 9, 1864. He was mustered on July 21, 1864, into the 42nd

Regiment Mass. Volunteer Infantry, Company D. He mustered out on November 11, 1864.

Warren Joy Vinal

Warren Vinal was born in Scituate on December 2, 1821, to Dexter and Eliza (Mott) Vinal. He was working as a shoemaker when he enlisted, at the age of 39, on September 10, 1861, as a private for three years. He was mustered on September 14, 1861, in the 1st Regiment Mass. Volunteer Cavalry, Company B. He did not receive a bounty. He was mustered out of the service on December 26, 1863. He reenlisted the same day, and was wounded on May 5, 1864, at Todd's Tavern, Virginia in the Battle of the Wilderness. He was transferred to the Veteran's Reserve Corps and mustered out on July 10, 1865.

Richard Walsh

Richard Walsh was born in Ireland and working as a laborer in Boston, when he enlisted, at age 19, and was mustered on December 14, 1864, as a private for one year. He served in the 26th Regiment Mass. Volunteer Infantry, Company C, and received a bounty of $100 from the town. He mustered out on August 26, 1865. He died in Boston in 1887 at the age of 57.

Galen Watson

Galen Watson was born in Boston on April 10, 1820, to Moses and Emma Watson. He was 44 and worked as a shoemaker, when he enlisted and mustered on August 9, 1864, into the 4th Regiment Mass. Volunteer Heavy Artillery, Company C as a private for three years. This unit served in defense of the City of Washington. He received a bounty of $125 from the town and $75 from a private donation. He mustered out on June 17, 1865, at Washington D.C.

Lemuel Webb

Lemuel Webb was born in Scituate on February 25, 1830, in Scituate to Lemuel and Lucy V. (Collier) Webb. He was a master mariner when he enlisted, at the age of 32, on August 14, 1862. He mustered on August 20, 1862, as a private for three years in the 39th Regiment Mass. Volunteer Infantry, Company C. He received a bounty of $100 from the town. He mustered out on June 2, 1865.

Marsena Webb Jr.

Marsena Webb was born in Scituate on May 30, 1826, to Marsena and Martha (Wood) Webb. He was working as carpenter when he enlisted at age 37, and mustered on August 10, 1864, into the 4th Regiment Mass. Volunteer Heavy Artillery, Company C, as a private for one year. He received a bounty of $125 from the town and $75 from a private donation. He mustered out on June 17, 1865, at Washington, D.C.

Thomas Richmond Webb

Thomas Webb was born in Scituate on May 3, 1828, a brother to Marsena. He was a shoemaker when he enlisted and mustered on August 10, 1864, at the age of 35. He mustered as a private for one year in the 4th Regiment Mass. Volunteer Heavy Artillery, Company C. He received a bounty from the town of $125 and a private donation of $75. He mustered out on June 17, 1865, at Washington D.C.

John Welch.

John Welch was born in Boston on August 22, 1838, to Robert and Matilda Welch. He worked as a mechanic and was living in Scituate when he enlisted and was mustered on June 15, 1861, as a private for three years in the 7th Regiment Mass. Regular Infantry, Company K. He was 22 years of age. He did not receive a bounty and was mustered out June 27, 1864, at Taunton, Massachusetts.

Nicholas Wherity

Nicholas Wherity was born in Ireland on May 12, 1844, to Patrick and Bridget Wherity. He was a fisherman and living in Scituate, when he enlisted and was mustered, at the age of 20, on October 23, 1861, as a private for three years in the 24th Regiment Mass. Volunteer Infantry, Company F. He was discharged on January 4, 1863, only to re-enlist again in the 24th Regiment Mass. Volunteer Infantry, Company F, again for three years. He was wounded on May 16, 1864, in the head by a minie ball at the Battle of Drury's Bluff on the James River. He recovered and was discharged on January 20, 1865. He was a member of Post 31 G.A.R.

William Henry Whipple

William Henry Whipple was a resident of Scituate and worked as a waiter. He enlisted on May 5, 1863 and mustered into service on May 12, 1863, as a private in the 54th Regiment Mass. Volunteer Infantry commanded by Robert Gould Shaw. William was wounded July 18, 1863, at Fort Wagner, South Carolina. He was discharged February 24, 1864, for wounds. William was listed as part of the town's quota in the Town Report year ending March 3, 1864, but not in *Scituate's Record of Names*. He is documented in the *Massachusetts Soldiers, Sailors, and Marines in the Civil War*.

George William Whitcomb

George Whitcomb was born in Cohasset on October 25, 1835, to David and Nancy C. Whitcomb. He was 28, living in Scituate and working as a bootmaker, when he enlisted and mustered on August 23, 1864, as a private for three years, in the 4th Regiment Mass. Volunteer, Company K. He received a bounty of $100 from the town. He was discharged on June 17, 1865, on a Surgeon's certificate of disability at a camp near Culpepper, Virginia.

William Johnson Whitcomb

William Whitcomb was born in Ashburnham on February 20, 1844, to Willard and Cynthia Whitcomb. He worked as a farmer. He enlisted and was mustered on June 15, 1861, as a private for three years in the 7th Regiment Mass. Volunteer Infantry, Company F. He was 18 years old. He died on March 20, 1862, at the Columbia College Hospital in Washington, D.C. after being sick for ten days with Typhoid Fever.

George Washington White

George White was born on October 10, 1840, in Stoughton, to Samuel and Mary White. He worked as a shoemaker. At the age of 23, he enlisted and was mustered on December 8, 1863, in the 39th Regiment Mass. Volunteer Infantry, Company G. as a private for three years. He did not receive a bounty. He was wounded on May 12, 1864, at Laurel Hill, Virginia. He was transferred in June 1865, to the 32nd Mass Vol. Infantry, Company C. He mustered out June 29, 1865. He also had enlisted earlier as George W. Wood at the age of 19 while living in Bridgewater, where he worked as a bootmaker. He enlisted and mustered on June 13, 1861, in the 11th Regiment Mass. Volunteer

Infantry, Company C. and apparently deserted on February 24, 1862, at the Battle of Budd's Ferry Maryland.

George Henry Whittaker

George Whittaker was born in Scituate on August 27, 1842, to John L. and Betsey Whittaker. He worked as a shoemaker when, at the age of 22, he enlisted on August 10, 1864. He mustered the same day in the 4th Regiment Mass. Volunteer Heavy Artillery, Company C as a corporal for one year. He received a bounty of $125 from the town and $72 from a private donation. He mustered out on June 17, 1865, at Washington D.C. He was a charter member of Post 31 G.A.R. He died in 1894 and is buried in Cudworth Cemetery.

Henry Wilson

Henry Wilson was born in Boston and at the age of 28, while working as a laborer he enlisted and mustered on May 18, 1864, for 1 year in the 2nd Regiment Mass. Volunteer Infantry as a private. He was paid a bounty of $125 by the town and by a private donation of $25. There is no record that he ever joined.

David Carver Witherell

David Witherell was born in Scituate on October 15, 1843, to Anson and Joanne M. (Jenkins) Witherell. He was a farmer. He enlisted at the age of 19 on August 4, 1862, as a private for 3 years. He mustered on August 20, 1862, in the 38th Regiment Mass. Volunteer Infantry, Company G. He received a bounty of $100 from the town. He was transferred to V.R.C. then retransferred to the 38th Mass. Volunteer Infantry on March 19, 1864. He was mustered out June 30, 1865.

Thomas A. Woodward

Thomas Woodward was a 28 year old from Athol, working as a mason, when he enlisted on the October 23, 1861, as a private for 3 years. Mustered on November 7, 1861, into the 15th Regiment Mass. Volunteer Heavy Artillery. He received a bounty of $125 from the town a $100 from a private source. He re-enlisted on January 1, 1864.

Charles Young

Charles Young was born in Scituate on March 31, 1831, to Gideon W. and Nancy (Mann)Young. He married in 1852 to Amelia Otis. He lived in Scituate and worked as printer when, at the age of 31, he enlisted on August 4, 1862, as a private for 3 years. He mustered on August 20, 1862, in the 38th Regiment Mass. Volunteer Infantry, Company G. He received a bounty of $100 from the Town. He was promoted to sergeant on May 5, 1863, and wounded in the fight at Port Hudson, Louisiana on June 14, 1863. He was detailed to the Telegraph Corps on April 28, 1864, and mustered out on July 2, 1865, as a sergeant. He was a member of Post 31 G.A.R.

Charles Drew Young

Charles Young was born in Weymouth, Mass. on July 2, 1832, to William and Dolly L. Young. He was living in Scituate and working as a mechanic when, at the age of 28, he enlisted, and mustered on June 15, 1861, as a corporal for 3 years in the 7th Regiment Mass. Volunteer Infantry, Company K. He mustered out on June 27, 1864, at Taunton Massachusetts.

Henry Young

Henry Young was born on March 31, 1834, in Scituate to Gideon Wade and Nancy Young Wade. He worked as a shoemaker when he enlisted, at age 39, on July 8, 1863, as a private for three years. He mustered on October 8, 1863, in the 2nd Regiment Mass. Volunteer Heavy Artillery, Company F. He did not receive a bounty. He mustered out on October 3, 1865. He was a member of Post 31 G.A.R. serving as Post Adjunct.

John Wesley Young Jr.

John Young was the son of John Wesley and Anna (Cook) Young. He worked as a laborer. At the age of 18, he enlisted and mustered on August 4, 1862, as a private for 3 years in the 38th Regiment Mass. Volunteer Infantry, Company G. He received a bounty of $100 from the town. He was discharged for disability at Baltimore, Maryland on December 27, 1862.

Men From Abington

On September 12, 1862, thirteen men from E. Abington (later Rockland) enlisted and mustered in the 43rd Regiment Mass. Volunteer Infantry, Company G. According to Wikipedia, at that time Abington was a major boot and shoe manufacturing town. Indeed, they provided nearly half the footwear provided for the Union Army during the Civil War. From 1846-1865 Abington was also, a center of the abolitionist movement.

This group included Ansell B. Randall, Andrew Rogers, Micah Rolland Shaw, Otis Richmond Shaw (he had served previously in the 60th Regiment Mass. Volunteer Infantry for 100 days), Solomon H. Shurtliff, Zenas Smith, David Stoddard (who reenlisted in Mass. 3rd Cavalry Regiment, Company M on January 5, 1864, and mustered out on January 25, 1865), George W. Stoddard, Andrew Hilton Studley, George L. Studley, (who reenlisted in the Mass. Heavy Artillery, Company A), Daniel F. Sullivan and Eugene Sullivan. Most of these men enlisted on August 28, 1862, and mustered on the September 12, 1862, in the 43rd Regiment Mass. Volunteer Infantry, Company G.

They all survived the War with the exception of Ansell Randall who was a dentist and after mustering out reenlisted in the 56th Infantry Regiment on December 12, 1863. He was promoted to full captain on May 17, 1864, and was killed at Petersburg Virginia at the Battle of Hatcher's Run on April 1, 1865, just two weeks before the surrender of General Robert E. Lee's Army of Northern Virginia to General Ulysses S. Grant's Army of the Potomac at Appomattox Court House.

These men were all credited to Scituate and monies were paid to the Town of Abington for their service.

Bibliography

Basler, Roy P. *Abraham Lincoln Speeches and Writings 1859-1865.* New York: The Library of America, 1989.

Briggs, Vernon L. *History of Shipbuilding on the North River with Genealogies of the Ship-builders Plymouth County, MA.* Boston: Coburn Brothers, Printers, 1889. Reprint Scituate, MA: Scituate Historical Society, 1970.

Catton, Bruce edited by James M. McPherson.*The American Heritage New History of the Civil War.* New York: Viking, 1988.

Civil War Facts. National Park Service U.S. Department of the Interior. Last modified February 27, 2015. http://www.nps.gov/civilwar/facts.htm.

Deane, Samuel. *History of Scituate, Massachusetts, From its First Settlement to 1831.* Boston: James Loring, 1831. Reprint, Scituate, MA: Scituate Historical Society, 1975.

Ellsworth, Edward W. (Wheelock College). *Massachusetts in the Civil*

War Volume III "The Year of Crisis" 1862-1863. Boston: Massachusetts Civil War Centennial Commission, 1962.

Fiore, Jordan D. (State College at Bridgewater). *Massachusetts in the Civil War Volume II "The Year of Trial and Testing" 1861-1862.* Boston: Massachusetts Civil War Centennial Commission, 1961.

Lincoln, Abraham. "Proclamation 83 – Increasing the Size of the Army and Navy." May 3, 1861. Online by Gerhard Peters and John T. Woolley, *The American Presidency Project.* Accessed March 24, 2015. http://www.presidency.ucsb.edu/ws/?pid=70123.

Lincoln, Abraham. "Executive Order." July 1, 1862. Online by Gerhard Peters and John T. Woolley, *The American Presidency Project.* Accessed March 24, 2015. http://www.presidency.ucsb.edu/ws/?pid=69811.

Lincoln, Abraham. "Executive Order." August 4, 1862. Online by Gerhard Peters and John T. Woolley, *The American Presidency Project.* Accessed March 26, 2015. http://www.presidency.ucsb.edu/ws/?pid=69818.

Lincoln, Abraham. "Proclamation 121 – Calling for 300,000 Volunteers." December 19, 1864. Online by Gerhard Peters and John T. Woolley, *The American Presidency Project.* Accessed April 2, 2015. http://www.presidency.uscb.edu/ws/?pid=70060.

Massachusetts Soldiers, Sailors and Marines in the Civil War Vol. I.-VIII Compiled and Published by The Adjutant General. Norwood, Mass.: Norwood Press, 1931.

Murphy, Barbara. *Irish Mossers and Scituate Harbour Village.* 1980.

Murphy, Barbara. *Scituate: The Coming of Age of a Plymouth Colony Town.* 1985.

O'Connor, Thomas H. *Massachusetts in the Civil War Volume I "The Call to Arms" 1860-1861.* Boston: Massachusetts Civil War Centennial Commission, 1960.

Oedel, Howard T. *Massachusetts in the Civil War Volume IV "A Year of Dedication" 1863-1864.* Boston: Massachusetts Civil War Centennial Commission, 1964.

Old Scituate. Chief Justice Chapter, Daughters of the American Revolution, 1921.

Post, Gerald. *First Guide to Civil War Genealogy and Research 3rd Edition*. Bloomington, Indiana: Trafford, 2010.

Pratt, Harvey Hunter. *The Early Planters of Scituate a History of the Town of Scituate, Massachusetts from its Establishment to the end of the Revolutionary War*. Published by the Scituate Historical Society, 1929.

Stower, Richard M. *A History of the First Parish Church of Scituate, Massachusetts: Its Life and Times*. Scituate, MA: Converpage.

Ward, Geoffrey C. with Ric Burns and Ken Burns. *The Civil War an Illustrated History*. New York: Alfred A. Knopf, 1990.

W.G.B. "Extract of a Letter." *The Liberator*, January 4, 1861.

Newspapers
The Hingham Journal and South Shore Advertisers. (Hingham Public Library)
The Liberator. (American Antiquarian Society, Worcester, Massachusetts)